DATE DUE

HIGHSMITH 45-220

El Gringo

El Gringo by D. H. RADLER

The Yankee Image in Latin America

CHILTON COMPANY · BOOK DIVISION · *Publishers*

PHILADELPHIA AND NEW YORK

Contents

El Gringo

Author's Note

Since 1958, Latin America has been home to me; as a natural result, I talk about it as "here." This usage will be familiar to newspaper readers, who are accustomed, in any story they read, to relating the word "here" to the dateline. And the dateline of this book is Latin America.

On the other hand, I am a gringo: my country is the United States of America; my people are those who call themselves "Americans" and whom everyone south of the border, being American also, calls "North Americans." Thus, when I use the words "we," "us," or "our," I am referring to my own country and my own people.

I doubt that these usages will cause confusion to the careful reader, and apologize in advance to those who may feel such confusion—pointing out that their sense of being pulled and hauled is assuredly no greater than my own as a gringo south of the border!

D. H. RADLER

La Esperanza, Honduras, C.A.

1

The Importance of Latin America

Throughout most of the history of the United States, it has been public policy to ignore the countries south of our own border. Even when that policy temporarily changed—in the Spanish-American War, for instance, and when we triggered a revolt to win the Panama Canal, and when our Marines were policing the Caribbean countries for us in the Big Stick era— North Americans in general remained nonchalantly unconcerned about, and reasonably ignorant of, Latin America.

Today, with the emergence of a Communist satellite in Cuba and the launching of the $20,000,000,000 Alliance for Progress, our Government has turned its eyes southward for the first time since the Roosevelt Good Neighbor days. But it is symptomatic of public lack of interest that, when the Cuban revolution broke out, we had not one scholar who had devoted his career to the study of that country to advise our government—and that, today, despite the clear-cut Communist threat in our hemisphere, most North Americans still view Latin America as an unimportant collection of laughable "banana republics."

Of course, our own cultural roots lie in Europe, as do the bodies of so many of our soldiers who fought there in World Wars I and II. But our Europe-oriented vision, coupled with blindness to other areas, allowed the Japanese sneak attack on Pearl Harbor in 1941 to succeed; permitted the Russians, once our allies, to gird themselves to become our most formidable enemies; laid the groundwork for the Korean War; and, latterly, opened up this hemisphere as a battleground in the Cold War.

3

That war is being fought now in Latin America. Little by little, it is being won by the Communists, despite the Alliance for Progress with its twenty billions. And most North Americans remain unconcerned about Latin America. Continuing unconcern could well mean the loss of half of "our" hemisphere.

What is that half of the hemisphere really like? Who are the people who live there? How do they think and feel? Where do they stand in the bipolar Cold War world? Where are they going?

These are not questions for which one can find answers on a one-month swing through the major South American capitals. Nor can answers be found in the official handouts of one or another Latin American government—because many of those governments do not represent their people, and because most of them are subject to change without notice. Instead, one must live with the Latin people, talk with them, listen to them. That is what I have been doing since 1958; it is from that richly rewarding—and sometimes shocking—daily experience that this book is drawn.

Latin America, as I use the term here, includes all the Spanish-speaking countries of this hemisphere plus Brazil, where Portuguese is the national language.[1] This encompasses an area two and a half times the size of Europe and a population already 20 million greater than that of the United States and soon to be double that of the United States. In size alone, an area of great importance to North Americans; and in proximity; and in many other regards as well.

The only water passage from the Atlantic to the Pacific is the Panama Canal; were this to be supplemented by another, it, too, would be in Latin America, either in Colombia's Río Atrato or in Lake Nicaragua. These real and potential canals need not belong to us (indeed, it would be better if they didn't, as we

[1] Mexico, Cuba, Guatemala, Honduras, Nicaragua, El Salvador, Costa Rica, Panama, Colombia, Venezuela, Ecuador, Peru, Chile, Paraguay, Uruguay, Bolivia, Argentina, Brazil, the Dominican Republic, and Puerto Rico. I exclude Haiti, British Honduras, and the European colonies in South America because of differences in history, culture, and language.

shall see in a later chapter), but they certainly must be in friendly hands. And as I have stated and will shortly set out to prove, the friendliness of those hands today is doubtful, at best.

Also in a strategic sense, we could not afford to have enemy bases established within our own hemisphere. Nor could we suffer the loss of certain essential materials now supplied entirely or nearly entirely by Latin America.[2]

Most important of all, however, is the political importance of Latin America in a world at war, even though that war be a "Cold War." There is, of course, no need to prove that such a war is in progress—current fevered construction of atom bomb shelters Stateside indicates full well my compatriots' awareness of the situation. But there may be need to mention the key role of Latin America today in that continuing world struggle.

Perhaps our southern neighbors need not be on our side, but we certainly cannot tolerate having them on the other side, as the example of Cuba has so uncomfortably demonstrated. Even those countries which are avowedly anti-Communist now serve as entry points for Communist agents, money, arms, and propaganda; should any of these countries become another Cuba—which could easily happen—that flow would be intensified. Furthermore, our prestige in the rest of the world depends on keeping our natural friends and closest neighbors in "the Western world." Any uncommitted, wavering nation can be expected to resolve its dilemma by joining what looks like the winning side. And if more nations in this hemisphere go over to the Communists . . . ?

These are, of course, arguments enough for the importance

[2] All of the sisal, henequen, and manila for naval ropes; all the quartz crystals for electronic use; 94 per cent of the mica; 91 per cent of the quality manganese ore; 96 per cent of the beryllium; 86 to 99 per cent of the tantalum; 90 per cent of the nickel; 91 per cent of the antimony; 100 per cent of the sodium nitrate. Also materials of economic value: all of the chicle, all of the ipecac, all of the carnauba wax, all of the carpet wool we use. And nearly all of the sperm whale oil, casein, balsa, mahogany, coffee, cocoa, sugar, and bananas (U.S. Department of Commerce, 1960).

to us of Latin America, but there are others of at least equal significance: the vast culture of this area, which we have largely ignored and from which we could derive much richness, and a way of life that has tremendous appeal.

Long before the Conquest, at least three advanced cultures existed here: the Mayas and Quichés of Mexico and Central America; the Aztecs of Mexico; and the Incas of Peru, Ecuador, and Bolivia.

The Mayas and Quichés flourished from the 4th to the 14th centuries as a peaceful, loosely knit group of city states ranging from southern Mexico to Guatemala and Honduras. Their outstanding achievements were their astronomical knowledge, unsurpassed in Europe until the 16th century, and their mathematical work, never bettered anywhere during their own time. It was the Mayas who invented the zero, centuries ahead of the Hindus; also to them is credited "position value coding," on the vigesimal rather than decimal system—not too unlike the basis of today's electronic computers.

(There is a delightful story about the Mayas' astronomical and mathematical skill by Augusto Monterroso Bonilla, the Guatemalan writer: Back in the days of the conquistadors, a monk from Spain becomes lost in the Guatemalan jungle. Stumbling around in all that vastness, he soon finds himself surrounded by a tribe of savages, complete with altar and blood-guttered sacrificial rock. Being a student of Aristotle, knowing that a solar eclipse is due that day, and hoping to frighten the Indians, he declares, "If you kill me, I will put out the sun." Two hours later, his blood is pouring out into the sacrificial stone; the eclipse is underway; and an Indian, in a dispassionate voice, is slowly reciting the dates of all upcoming solar and lunar eclipses, which the Mayas had long ago calculated and written in their codices—without benefit of Aristotle.)

The Aztecs, a warlike people, established themselves in the Mexican valley of Anáhuac, where Mexico City now is, in the 13th century or earlier. By the 16th century they dominated a large part of what is now Mexico and some of Central America. Fanatically religious, they practiced human sacrifice

6

on a grand scale, basing the bloody rite on the fact that the Sun, "god that he is, disdains the gross food that men eat and can only sustain himself on life itself, the magic substance that is found in the blood of man."[3]

But their religion also dictated the adoption of the older Mexican Indian practice of pyramid-building and of elaborate sculpture in stone; several of their pyramids were greater in volume than the Egyptian, and much of their sculpture was on a par with the best of the Old World.

The Incas, who included all the nations of the Quechua language, already represented a formidable empire by the 12th century. The limits of that empire are still unknown, but traces of it exist in Peru, Chile, Ecuador, and Argentina. To facilitate the governing of such a vast territory, the Incas developed a sophisticated economic system and a great ability in the statistics of population, maintaining a head count, town by town and farm by farm, that is still not equaled today by any civilized country. Further, they united Cuzco, the capital, with every part of the empire, by roads and bridges far better than any in the Europe of their time.

These developments are especially impressive when one considers that the Incas never developed writing: their records were kept on complicated bunches of knotted strings (*quipus*); their engineering planning was performed with three-dimensional models similar to those that architects derive today from their blueprints.

The Conquest destroyed almost all of this development and superimposed Christianity and Spanish culture on the pre-existing Indian civilizations. As we shall see later in this chapter and throughout this book, that overlay proved fairly flimsy in many cases. But it can be said that the culture of Latin America since the Conquest is the product of the indigenous and the Spanish—and, in general, it is a fine product.

Skipping from pre-Conquest times to our own days (and

[3] Mexican archeologist Alfonso Caso, as quoted in Pedro Henríquez Ureña, *Historia de la Cultura en la América Hispánica,* Fondo de Cultura Económica, Mexico, 1959 (4th edition).

thereby giving short shrift to poets like Cuba's José Martí and Nicaragua's Rubén Darío and writers such as Brazil's Machado de Assis), Latin America has been and is producing an outpouring of creativity that ranks with the best in the world, albeit the attention we pay it is slim indeed. The art of Mexico—Diego Rivera, Orozco, Siqueiros, and Tamayo—is, of course, well known and widely respected, and has had tremendous influence on our own modern realistic painting. But it is equaled and in some cases surpassed by the work of Brazil's Cándido Portinari, Ecuador's Egas, Peru's Sabogal, Codesido, and Blas, Honduras' López Rodezno and Mario Castillo, and many more. (Should you wish to compare the work of some of these painters with ten of our leading contemporary artists, order Volume IV, Number 25, *Artes de Mexico,* from the National University, Mexico City.)

In literature, Latin America in recent years has produced poets, novelists, short story writers, and essayists to rank with the world's very best. Take, for example, the poetry and prose of Gabriela Mistral of Chile (Nobel prize for literature, 1945), or the poetry, rich in startling new images, of Mexico's Alfonso Reyes, Chile's Pablo Neruda, Argentina's Jorge Luís Borges, and Peru's César Vallejo, whose life and work we shall analyze in a later chapter. Or the essays, sound and biting, of Brazil's Gilberto Freyre and Colombia's Germán Arcienegas. Or the revolutionary novels of Mexico's Martín Luís Guzmán.

In journalism, my own view of Latin America's press as superior to that of the United States is seconded by Professor Ronald Hilton, director of Latin American studies at Stanford, who has said, "A study of the U.S. press demonstrates that there are few papers to compare in quality with 'Excelsior' of Mexico, except 'The New York Times.'" Indeed, we have little besides the "good, gray Times" to compare with either *Excelsior* or the leading papers of Rio de Janeiro, Buenos Aires, and Santiago de Chile. And the smaller papers here, such as Costa Rica's *La Nación,* Honduras' *El Día,* and Guatemala's *Imparcial* are head and shoulders above the press of com-

8

parable size in the States in range, completeness, and accuracy of coverage, to say nothing of editorial acumen and courage. As James A. Wechsler, editor of *The New York Post,* has pointed out, "Most of the deans of the profession are now alternately engaged in mutual admiration exercises . . . and the discovery of safe postures which spare them any conflict with large advertisers or commanders of the American Legion."[4]

The language barrier prevents our appreciating Latin American literature and journalism. In painting, there is no such obstacle, nor is there in music. We are able to consume Latin American music without technical difficulties, and we have done so, although the usual rendition Stateside, lacking the rhythmic and harmonic subtleties, is a fairly pale imitation. (I always believed Latin American music was no better than the three-chord nonmusic of our hillbillies—until I came here and heard the real thing.) Despite our having adopted much of the prodigious production of Mexico's Agustín Lara ("Granada," "Mujer," "Noche Criolla," etc.), the "Malagueña" of Cuba's Ernesto Lecuona, and much of the classical composition of Brazil's Heitor Villa-Lobos, we have missed almost completely the work of Carlos Chávez of Mexico and the mature, splendid creations of his compatriot, Manuel M. Ponce. Ponce's "Concierto del sur" for guitar and orchestra, as played by Segovia, is a listening experience I recommend to anyone with ears.

Speaking of music, I would like to introduce a personal observation: that it is difficult to find a Latin American who does not make some kind of music on a guitar. Gypsy that I am, I forsook piano for guitar some years ago, in the interest of portability. My Goya hangs on the wall in the living room. People come to visit. They all want to try that beautiful instrument. And they all get something out of it, down to our current yardboy, a Lenca Indian who can hardly speak Spanish, stubby-fingered like most of his race, with a memory shorter than his little finger. And yet he plays—Mexican rancheras

4 James A. Wechsler, *Reflections of an Angry Middle-Aged Editor,* Random House, 1960.

and Spanish boleros—all with a sense of rhythm that is perfect and an unself-conscious grace that is beautiful to see. Admittedly, he plays when he should be working. But he plays.

More and more, science has become the prevailing culture in the United States, bringing with it a refreshing wave of rationalism, at least in certain quarters. Research, especially industrial research, is much less widespread in Latin America. But this area has its successes in science for all that, including the physiological studies of Argentina's Bernardo Alberto Houssay (Nobel prize in medicine, 1947), the cosmic ray research of Mexico's Sandoval Vallarta, the biological studies of Peru's Carlos Monge, the anthropological work of Peruvians J. Urciel García and Julio C. Tello, Mexicans Manuel Gamio and Alfonso Caso and Argentine Félix Faustino Outes, the archeological studies of Ecuador's Jacinto Jijón y Caamaño, and the ethnological work of Brazil's Ulises Pernambucano and Arthur Ramos, and Cuba's Fernando Ortíz.

Much of the work and many of the names I have mentioned are unknown in the States, or, at best, familiar only to specialists or to that group whose interest is dictated as much by the urge to be different as by any legitimate cultural range. On the other hand, the art, music, literature, journalism, and science of the United States is well known here—in some cases, to our definite disadvantage—and much of it is copied here, often to the disadvantage of the Latins. Cultural exchange between the United States and Latin America has been, in fact, pretty much of a one-way street, and this is one of the many reasons we are not popular here.

In the States, as John Kenneth Galbraith has pointed out, production has become, or, better said, has remained beyond the point of usefulness, a fetish: the North American is work-oriented.[5] From this accent on getting the job done comes much of the social syndrome known as organization-worship. Included in this syndrome are the symptoms of "other-direction" (Riesman), "organization man-ism" (Whyte), being subject to

[5] John Kenneth Galbraith, *The Affluent Society,* Houghton Mifflin Company, 1958.

10

the tastemakers (Lynes), and the wastemakers (Packard) and, in general, conformity (everybody). To achieve success, or what passes for success, the North American man must dedicate himself to his work; usually, the higher he rises, the greater becomes his dedication. It is in no way unusual for a man who "has arrived" to leave his home in Park Forest, Ill., or Danbury, Conn., at seven in the morning, not to return until the same hour, or later, at night. Meanwhile, the daily life of his household goes on without him—his children eat, study, play, pray, and sleep in quite another world. This is the pattern of Suburbia and Exurbia, the pattern that is fast becoming the norm for all North America. Its results can be seen in the divorce courts, in the delinquency statistics, in the psychiatrist's office, and, more than anywhere, in the popular literature, from comic strips to slicks. Daddy (Dagwood, let us say) may be quite an important man downtown, but he is pretty much of a loss as a human being: it is in Mother's hands that the reins of the family—and the family funds—lie. Daddy (any one of the middle-aged males in *Redbook, Cosmopolitan,* and *McCall's*) just is not in the picture at all: he is too busy working. Even *Jack and Jill,* the magazine for tots, notes the trend: "My favorite writer? My Daddy. He writes checks!"

In contrast with this, the Latin man, whether he wields a machete or a mortgage is first and foremost a family man. For him, no amount of professional fame or esteem can offset having a stupid or lazy or criminal son, just as no business crisis can ever interfere with a family affair such as a wedding, a baptism, a birthday, an illness, a death, or the anniversary of death. I have often seen major political and business figures leave the capital every year to perform the rites of this latter anniversary back in their home towns.

The other side of the production coin is consumption, and we worship heads and tails alike. Prestige is a bigger car, a second TV set, a third radio; success is the ability to consume, more and more, faster and faster. We see ourselves as idealists, and indeed, in anything of secondary importance, such as making friends in the rest of the world, we are idealists. But Latin

11

Americans see us as the crassest of materialists, warped under a value system measured, not in cultural achievements, not in friends won, but in dollars spent. (I do not believe that my compatriots, in reality, worship the Almighty Dollar, although they seem to the rest of the world to do just this. Instead, they revere the acts of producing and consuming for their own sake; they are thing-oriented rather than dollar-oriented.)

On the other hand, given a choice between some overtime or a hunting trip, between another 10 per cent gain or a bull session on art, politics, and religion, the Latin man will usually choose the latter. In part (but only in small part) that is one of the reasons these are among the hungry nations. But it is also why they are among the happy nations.

Take, for example, some sights I saw not long ago in Mexico. Not the Mexico of the guidebooks and the 78 dollar tours, of peons lounging in the hot sun, of chili peppers and fried worms, of bullfights and mañana. Not the tourist's Mexico, but the real Mexico.

I was in Cuernavaca, fleeing from the gray skies and chill air of the city, which is just half a mile too high for me. I went into the state capital (Cuernavaca may be just a distant suburb of Mexico City, but it is also the capital of the State of Morelos) to look at the Diego Rivera murals.

But I never really saw them: heads and shoulders kept getting in the way. Tourists? There wasn't one. These were *campesinos,* shirt-sleeved farmers, many without shoes. There was a constant stream of them. And they all behaved the same way: they would climb up the old iron staircase, turn the corner, and encounter one end of the murals. Then they would look up to see how far these huge paintings extended, shaking their heads in wonder at the sheer scope of the work. They would walk to dead center, step back, and look. Only it was more than a look—as the Spanish language points out, a look is to throw, and they were catching. Catching and holding and absorbing all that sweep of color and line, drinking in the hard history of their country that it portrays, and growing a little. In silence,

12

drinking the paint from the walls as if it were still wet and flowing.

Then they would walk close, concentrating on some detail, and then back again, and then, hesitantly, dragging their eyes along like reluctant children, they would leave. Just before they reached the stairs again they would extend tentative fingers, touch the painted wall ever so delicately, reverently, and then they would go. Taking with them a memory of beauty that was now part of them, just as their dark eyes and swarthy skin and work-toughened hands are part of them.

I took a picture of the murals, letting the straw hats and the bulky shoulders of these men serve as frame. Everybody who sees the picture comments on the men, not the murals, and I guess that is what I was doing when I shot it. I never met Diego Rivera, but I'll wager a long weekend in Cuernavaca that he would have preferred the accent on the people instead of on the painting, too.

Duty (such a dirty word!) dragged me back to the city and, as luck would have it, past the Palace of Fine Arts. Alongside the *Palacio* is a huge bookstore, and attached to the bookstore are loudspeakers, and through the loudspeakers comes classical music. Standing all around are blue-collar workers, city cousins of the *campesinos* I saw in Cuernavaca, listening to the music. It is strangely hushed in that little verdant patch, because no one is talking—and that, around any Latins, is a phenomenon. Everyone is listening to the music, not just hearing it, but listening to it. And sometimes a man walks, quietly, closer to the bookstore, as if he might see within the men who are making the music, the violinists, the flutists, the tympanists who let you know why you have ears.

Wondering whether these people knew what they were hearing (not that that is really important; many people can follow a score with the best of them but don't like music), I started to approach the man nearest me. Before I could open my mouth he whispered, "Ah, *señor,* that 'Botch'!" They knew, all right. . . .

They might have been late for work, those art-rapt Mexicans, or they might have been out of work: there are plenty of unemployed in Mexico, just as there are all over Latin America. But for the moment, at least, they were happy, as happy as we can be with a new Caddy, and when they got home it was "those big murals" or "that music—¡caramba!" that they told their wives and kids about, thereby launching another generation that can live on not much more than rice, beans, tortillas, talk, and beauty.

Admittedly, had I been surrounded by this degree of art appreciation in Central America, I would not even have noticed it when I hit Mexico. The latter country, along with Brazil and Argentina, probably leads the hemisphere in popular attachment to things beautiful. And this brings us to another consideration that is too often overlooked when we talk about Latin America—its incredible range of social, economic, religious, racial, and even linguistic differences. There are not too many more people here than there are in the States, but their diversity is astounding, far surpassing the differences between a New York doctor of the Jewish faith and a Georgia farmer who attends the Baptist church. The New Yorker and the Georgian can, at least, communicate; in time of war, they can and do serve side by side.

Not so Latin Americans.

To begin with, Brazil, with half the total population of South America, 60,000,000 people, speaks Portuguese rather than Spanish. Speaks it proudly, nearly exclusively, and with something of a prejudice, in fact, against the use of Spanish.

As for the rest of the area—in which Spanish is the official language—what differences exist! Casual students are fond of saying that Latin American Spanish differs from that of Spain in that the letters *z* and *c* are pronounced, in the former, as *s* and in the latter, as *th*. This is not exactly true, inasmuch as many Spaniards, including Andalusians, Catalans, Valencianos, Basques, and those of the Canary Islands, say it as *s*. More serious students note that the *ll* sound of the Spanish of Spain has become, in Latin America, *y*. But it has not, at least in large

14

areas of Colombia (where the world's best Spanish is spoken), of Ecuador, Peru, Chile, and Argentina. And in much of Central America, not only does *ll* as such exist, but even *y* has such a strong sound that the pronoun *yo* often comes out *Joe.* Yet the *ll has* given way to *y* in Andalusia, in large parts of Castile, and in the common idiom of Madrid.

There are five somewhat overlapping speech zones in Latin America, aside from the unique zone that is Brazil: (1) Mexico and Central America; (2) the Caribbean area, including the Antilles and the coasts of Venezuela and Colombia; (3) the Andean region, including part of Venezuela, most of Colombia, Peru, Bolivia, and northeast Argentina; (4) Chile; (5) the Río Plata area, which encompasses most of Argentina and all of Uruguay and Paraguay.[6]

But even within these zones, there are differences of rhythm, of accent, and even of words—sometimes to a traveler's discomfort. I remember trying to buy a bedspread in Panama. I was offered, respectively, a pack of Camels, a Brownie Kodak, and a toy camel—until I explained that *"camera"* is something you put on a bed. "But that," the pretty salesgirl told me, "is *sobrecama.* Wherever did you get that funny word *camera?"* "Honduras," I said, and laughed as she shook her head over those silly Indians up north!

But it's all Spanish, more or less, and one can make himself understood throughout the area—more or less. Until he enters one of the many zones where Spanish still has not supplanted the Indian language. And these zones are many, vast, and, despite years of effort by governments, missionaries, and others, seemingly unchangeable. For example, in Mexico today there are still over a million Indians who have not learned Spanish; most speak Náhuatl, the Aztec tongue. In Bolivia, the majority speak Aymara or the Inca language, Quechua, instead of Spanish; in Chile, a third of a million people speak Araucana (but most of these also speak Spanish); in Paraguay, Guaraní is spoken outside of the capital, but again, most of the people also speak Spanish; in Guatemala, over half the population

6 Pedro Henríguez Ureña, op. cit.

15

speak Quiché rather than Spanish. Beyond these major groups, there are throughout the area pockets of population in which tens of thousands speak one or another of the lesser Indian tongues. In the Atlantic littoral of Honduras and Nicaragua, Mosquitia is spoken, and in the southwestern highlands of Honduras into El Salvador the Guayijíqui Indians speak Lenca.

(Strange as these names may sound, the languages are not entirely unknown to us. Our cocoa, coyote, chicle, chili, chocolate, and tomato come from the Náhuatl; alpaca, condor, guano, llama, puma, and vicuña are from the Quechua; ipecac, jaguar, petunia, tapioca, and tapir are from the Guaraní.)

These language differences testify to the high percentage of indigenous peoples in the areas mentioned; *their* Latin America is more Indian than Latin. (And, recently, the Communist press here is taking advantage of that fact by calling the area "Indian America," thereby highlighting the differences between Latin Americans and North Americans and putting the political struggle on a racial basis.) Contrast this with such countries as Argentina, whose people are predominantly white and whose residents of the Federal Capital and Province of Buenos Aires (nearly half the population) are almost exclusively of European origin; Uruguay, where there are no native Indians left and only 10 per cent are mestizos, the mixture of Indian and European; and Costa Rica, over 90 per cent of whose people are of European origin.

We think of Latin America as Catholic in religion, but here again there is tremendous diversity. The non-Spanish speaking Indians for the most part have not adopted the white man's gods any more readily than they have his language. And among the bulk of the Indian population—even those of Spanish speech and nominal Catholicism—the new religion is overlaid on the old, often with charming effect: the Holy Trinity is worshiped—but it also represents the old gods with the old names. And they are helped by a host of lesser gods and spirits, all of whose names are invoked in whispers in the midst of a supposedly Catholic mass.

Peruvian architect Héctor Velardo enjoys telling of the In-

16

dians of a rich village who asked him to build a church for them. "We are Christians," they assured him, "and we want a Christian church. But could you bring in Sun worship somehow?"

I have seen the Lenca Indians of Honduras and El Salvador trooping to the church for Mass—and bringing with them their masked holy men, their Panpipes, their ritual drums. They enter the church in the order prescribed by their old religion (and if all twelve holy men, representing the twelve major gods are not present, they do not enter at all); they pray first in normal Christian form and then in ancient rites to "the Black Christ," symbol of the pure Lenca Indian. Then, on the steps of the church, they perform a Passion play of the Stations of the Cross —but with the use of masks and pipes and drums the play approaches ancient superstition more closely than modern religion.

It is true that most of Latin America is officially Catholic— but in Uruguay, the church is disestablished and Easter Week is called Tourist Week; and in Mexico, the Constitution of 1917, which severely restricts the activities of the church, has been jealously maintained by every government since that date. Mexicans follow the church in religious matters, but the majority fear its influence in mundane affairs. Under the 1917 Constitution, all church property was expropriated by the State; primary education was similarly treated; monastic orders were outlawed, and even the wearing of religious habits was forbidden (the latter injunction has not been enforced for some time, but is still extant); State legislatures were given the power to determine how many priests were allowed in their territory (and, some years ago, the legislature of the State of Tabasco allowed only one—and only if he were married!).

There are countries in which most of the population cannot read or write, such as Honduras and Nicaragua; others in which nearly everyone is literate, such as Argentina, Uruguay, and Costa Rica; and the entire range in between. There are countries still in the grip of a dictator, such as Paraguay, Nicaragua, and, once again, Cuba; there are democracies that have

17

solved the "color problem" better than we, such as Brazil; there is Uruguay, a long-term welfare state; Mexico, a democracy in which the same party always wins the elections; El Salvador, governed now by an elected president, now by a military junta that ousted him, but always by the famous and powerful "Fourteen Families."

There are tropical countries and temperate ones; steamy jungles à la Hollywood and brisk, sometimes bone-chilling highlands. There are areas of industrial boom, such as Brazil's São Paulo, and sleepy agricultural lands like Nicaragua. There are severely overpopulated lands, such as El Salvador, and areas virtually untrod by human feet, such as Brazil's Amazon Basin (one twentieth of the world's land area!).

A big, diverse, confusing place, Latin America, and not one for which any single policy can be forged and applied with any hope of success. Yet out of this bigness and diversity, coupled with its closeness to home for North Americans, comes top priority importance. Also, to one who feels affinity with a culture in which diversity supplants conformity and a way of life in which time is not money but something to enjoy in and for itself, a marvelous place to live in and to know.

2

Our Past Failures in Latin America

An important place, Latin America; a fascinating place. And here we have failed.

In mid-1958, *Time* magazine assured its readers of "the strongest proof so far that the U.S. can still count on a deep reservoir of good will south of the border." (This "proof" was applause for Milton Eisenhower in the Costa Rican legislature!) When he returned from his Central American tour, Dr. Eisenhower submitted a report to his President-brother. It differed, a bit, from what *Time* had said. Items: ". . . now I must add a note of urgency . . ." ". . . misunderstandings seem to me to be even more serious than they were in 1953." "In Latin America, misunderstandings of our policies, programs and attitudes are pervasive"[1]

Dr. Eisenhower and not *Time* magazine was apparently right, for soon after came the Cuban Revolution and the hottest wave to date of anti-Yanqui feeling throughout Latin America.

Before that revolution, it was fairly standard for our press to explain the difficulties between us and Latin America on the basis that we were big, rich, and powerful and, therefore, envied—and to minimize the difficulties themselves. But even after that revolution, such papers as *The Miami Herald* were playing down the conflicts and using the "rich uncle" bit to explain them away. And as recently as September 28, 1961, Gladys Delmas, writing in *The Reporter,* which stands at al-

[1] "United States-Latin American Relations; Report to the President," by Dr. Milton S. Eisenhower, U.S. Department of State, Washington, December 27, 1958.

most the opposite pole from *Time,* declared: ". . . it cannot be said that Mexicans themselves, either officials or the man in the street, have altered their attitude toward us, which is, as always, compounded of warm liking and a certain wariness toward a powerful neighbor."[2]

In the interim between *Time's* rosy report and *The Reporter's* equally cheerful misstatement, we had made new enemies in these parts with our ill-conceived and miserably managed Cuban invasion attempt, plans for which were reportedly approved without dissent by a top-level special committee headed by President Kennedy himself. (The complete failure of the invasion in specific military terms, as well as in terms of our public relations throughout Latin America, testified to our unawareness of the real conditions in Cuba at that time and of the image any invasion attempt, successful or not, would create throughout this part of the world.) And Adlai Stevenson had reported to President Kennedy that economic conditions, political stability, and respect for the United States were weakening in South America, while discontent and pro-Communist sentiment were on the rise.

Press coverage of Latin America in the United States is pitifully limited, generally poor, and occasionally quite damaging to us. And this poor coverage allows diplomatic errors, unreported, to be repeated, as I shall show in Chapter 3. But this coverage, whether it be the institutionalized irresponsibility of *Time's* Latin American edition or the prize-winning reportage of *The Reporter,* shares one bias—to tell North Americans that Latins really love 'em, revolutions, embassy attacks, effigy- and flag-burning notwithstanding.

There are, of course, exceptions. But in general, our press plays down the ugly face of the United States in Latin America if it covers the area at all, thereby fostering a dangerous complacency among our already perilously smug public.

The facts are as Dr. Eisenhower and Governor Stevenson reported them. Our policies, procedures, and personnel are not

[2] Gladys Delmas, "Mexico: The Middle-Aged Revolution," *The Reporter,* September 28, 1961.

widely understood or admired here; our usual attempts to explain them are quite uniformly shrugged off as propaganda, making matters all the worse. The five succeeding chapters cite specific examples of our diplomatic, business, press, "expert," and tourist behavior in Latin America to account for our widespread lack of popularity. Meanwhile, here is evidence, from personal experience and from certain significant writings and statistics, to support Dr. Eisenhower and Governor Stevenson.

The key is Fidel Castro. For many, many Latins his revolution was popular because it was against a dictator we had supported and *against the domination of his small country by our business interests.* Since then, Fidel has betrayed his own battle, turning the Pearl of the Antilles over to even worse foreign domination, and many Latins who had worshiped him now despise him.

and who forced him to do it?

But others don't. As of early 1962, after the Punta del Este meeting at which the Castro regime was censured, Fidel's picture still occupied the place of honor in many Latin homes, alongside that of Christ and supplanting those of such local heroes as Morazán and Bolívar. You'll find it in the *manaca* shacks of banana workers in Honduras, Guatemala, and Panama; on the adobe walls of coffee workers in El Salvador and Costa Rica; on the galvanized iron walls of oil workers in Venezuela, and miners in Chile and Bolivia, in the little shops and bars of the poor all over Latin America. Folded, grimy, and worn from much looking, it's found in the pockets of Cuban *guajiros,* Colombian *llaneros,* and *campesinos* everywhere. Tell them their President is a fool and they'll agree or disagree; that the church is sucking their blood and they'll listen and discuss. But don't say too harsh a word against Fidel, even now, if you don't want to duck a well-aimed machete. (And these are the facts that caused Castro to receive, at Punta del Este, no more than a slap on the wrist, because six nations at the conference, including the largest—Mexico, Brazil, Argentina, and Chile—abstained.)

There is a little restaurant where my family eats quite often, run by a woman three of whose sons are students of

21

mine in the local high school. We are always welcomed with warm *abrazos;* there is always a special something for Jeannie, my wife—a new herb tea or tortillas with chicharrones, one of her favorites. The young girl of the family, my daughter's age, spends more time at our house than she does at home. Good friends and good neighbors; we've helped each other out in many ways quite often.

But the other night, an educational supervisor from the capital was eating there, and the talk turned to Fidel. This family was for him, all the way. "But he's a Communist!" the visitor said. "That doesn't matter," said the eldest son (star pupil of my fourth course), "he threw the gringos out!" Then he flushed, embarrassed and probably thinking of his final grade, but he went on gamely, "Well, he did."

The point is that these people are polite; they know what side their tortillas are buttered on; maybe they like my family and maybe they don't. But they *don't* like gringos in general, and we never would have known it until Dr. Castro was mentioned.

Sometimes it comes out without Fidel. I recall the case of a small company whose manager was a gringo. He was always treated with respect, warmth, even, and when he left, the workers organized a combination farewell and protest meeting, urging him to stay on. He was replaced by a local man— and suddenly, the running spate of labor troubles that had plagued the company for years disappeared. In the local jokes, the ones they tell in the streets, his name, stripped of the honorific "Meester," began to appear quite prominently. Today those jokes are so current that just the mention of the name brings a snicker.

And there was the time we were sitting around in my study, fiddling with some rich gray clay my boys had found in the hills and brought home for modeling. With us was a good friend, a teacher and writer and—rarity among Latin intellectuals—a nonpolitical person, a neutralist on philosophical grounds. We had a few drinks and played with the clay some more, and then I looked at what Juancito was modeling. It was an Indian,

22

doubled over in a position of submission under a huge cowboy boot—the boot of Yanqui imperialism in Latin America. Seeing my gaze move to the crude but effectively worked little figure, Juancito followed it with his own, and reddened. "I didn't realize what I was making," he said. "It just came out . . ."

The incident turned out well rather than badly—Juancito later admitted to a lifelong anti-Yanqui feeling that he himself hadn't been fully aware of, and, discussing it with us, lost much of it and became an even better friend than before. Soon he became the source of new insights into the relationships between Latins and gringos.

Not all my experiences have been this gentle and philosophical. I've looked down the barrel of a .38 that seemed a young cannon; I've occasionally found it necessary to carry a pistol myself. I've ducked a machete; I've been called every kind of a gringo from *pendejo* to *jueputa*. These incidents invariably involved people who had had more drinks than they could handle, taking out their grudge against gringos in general by attacking the first one they met. But every time this has happened I've had other Latins intervene on my behalf, sometimes at significant personal risk. And almost every time the difficulty has been resolved after a cup of coffee and some conversation.

(All of this could have been avoided if I had stayed away from the places where such incidents could be expected, of course. But then I never would have learned how gringo is linked with other epithets here, the way Yankee is preceded by "damn" in our South. Or known the after-work face of the poor. These sights and sounds are the part of Latin America our diplomats and reporters don't see; they neither talk with the people in their own language, nor go where the people, in the sense of the poor and bitter majority, spend their time. Furthermore, the official position a diplomat holds, or the press card a reporter flashes, automatically puts Latins on guard, as they are on guard even with their own officials. When one of our official representatives here tells you this book exaggerates anti-Yanqui feelings, ask him how he knows. . . .)

Regarding the violence, this is not as so many of our experts might have it, "hot Latin blood." Many parts of Latin America are today similar to our old frontier West, with official law scarce and one's only protection carried in pocket or holster. There is violent crime, official negligence and dishonesty, crude and sometimes cruel justice—or misjustice. These are not commendable traits here or anywhere else, but they are characteristic of any emerging democracy. It is symptomatic of a little psychological astigmatism on our part that we idolize our early gunslingers on TV and in movies, meanwhile clucking puritanically over "those hotheaded Latins"—especially when we are always careful to point out that Latin America is underdeveloped. The violence is, of course, merely one of the social characteristics of underdevelopment, one we ourselves manifested and now enjoy in vicarious retrospect.

You don't have to accept the existence of strong anti-gringo feeling from my statements alone. Look in the literature. As early as 1872, in his epic poem about the gaucho, "Martin Fierro," Argentine poet José Hernandez wrote the line, "How big and ugly is the gringo!" Then, in 1900, when theater in Argentina and Uruguay lost its itinerant, circus-like quality and settled down into what we know as cosmopolitan theater, gaucho stories gave way to sophisticated comedies—and the most popular of all was Uruguayan Florencio Sánchez' "La Gringa." Not much later, Manolo Cuadra of Nicaragua was writing stories like "The Tortured Ones," in which the torturers are gringos, and Victor Cáceres Lara, a Honduran, was producing works like "Malaria," in which the villain is one of our banana countries. Since the 1940's, Chilean Poet Pablo Neruda, a Communist youth leader in his own country, has been writing poems like "The Advocates of the Dollar," "Standard Oil Co." "Anaconda Mining Co.," and "United Fruit Company," all consonant with the Communist line, of course, but all revelatory of our errors and all quite popular throughout Latin America.

But literature, like personal experience, is a fairly subtle thing. Let's look at it in concrete terms—the statistics of buy-

24

ing and selling. Here is a direct quote from the April 5, 1960 issue of *Noticias,* published by our National Foreign Trade Council:

"U.S. '59 exports to Latin America dropped 15% to $3,495 million worth from $4,073 million in '58, with sales of nearly all major commodities falling; electrical machinery exports, especially those to Cuba, Mexico and Argentina, dropped sharply; shipments of other types of machinery also dipped, with sizeable decreases in those to Venezuela, Brazil and Mexico; exports of railroad transportation equipment, aircraft and automobiles, parts & accessories were down, as were shipments of iron & steel-mill products and finished metal manufactures. . . ."

From the same publication, May 3, 1960: "Brazil: Soviet trade mission arrives in republic to work out details of a 3-year, $100 million trade pact. . . ." "Chile: Govt. reportedly is studying the feasibility of marketing copper in Soviet-bloc countries in cash & barter transactions . . . in return [4 East European nations] offer copper ore concentration plants, a copper refinery, coal mining equipment, agricultural products and hydroelectric facilities . . ." "Colombia: Czech Skoda works reportedly is ready to lend $25 million to Colombian firm Panal to assemble Skoda vehicles in Bogotá. . . ." "Argentina: Of the $100 million credit negotiated by Argentina in '58 for the purchase of Soviet machinery, by last February orders had been placed for over $32 million worth of oil-drilling and transport equipment. . . ." "Metals & Minerals: Poland offers to build a steel mill in Brazil with a 150,000-ton yearly capacity; will accept payment in Brazilian products over 8 years."

A year later (April 4, 1961) *Noticias* reported: "Net increase in U.S. direct private investments in Latin America last year amounted to $93 million, compared to $205 million in '59, while the net increase in Latin American capital in the U.S. was $23 million as against $102 million in '59."

It is difficult to get comparative figures of any reliability, especially since Soviet statistics tend to be shaded to their own propaganda advantage. But on balance, it appears that our

25

dollar dealings with Latin America have fallen some 15 per cent in the past two years, while those of Russia and her satellites have risen the same amount. In other words, the business flow is leaving us and going to them.

This, I believe, is about as concrete a manifestation as one could have of accelerating disenchantment with the United States, especially in view of the fact that in general our products and techniques are superior to those of Russia and her satellites and no more costly. Less costly, actually, if one takes transportation into account. It also leads to the most unpleasant political consequences, since every "technical expert" and "repairman" sent here by Red firms doing business with Latin America is a real or potential spy, agent provocateur, or propagandist, as we shall see in detail in Chapter 8.

CUBA

I was there while Batista was still running the show and while Castro was still bringing his revolution into the final stages. One night I especially remember—twenty of Batista's bully boys were killed and their bodies left lying in the streets of Havana. It was a nation ripe for revolution, overripe; its people had had all they wanted of being pushed around; every bar and restaurant and street corner was a meeting place for conspirators and revolutionaries.

Yet our State Department apparently knew nothing of this, or paid it little heed; our Ambassador was one of Batista's big chums, as his predecessor had been before him. When Fidel swept in, it came as an uncomfortable surprise for us—our press and public as well as our Government—and for a long time we didn't know what to make of Fidel. Then our CIA demonstrated its astuteness by assuring us that Fidel was not a Communist—and a few months later, the first Western Hemisphere nation to enter the Red orbit was officially announced. (Combine this early intelligence failure with the later and larger one concerning the Cuban invasion flop and you wonder how much our "experts" know about Cuba. And Cuba is only 90 miles away—what about Brazil, Chile, and Argentina?)

Current events are, of course, history updated, and the Cuban Revolution is no exception. To understand that revolution, we must examine a little of Cuba's sad history.

Discovered by Columbus on his first voyage in 1492, Cuba belonged to itself until 1511, when Diego Velázquez and 300 Spanish soldiers arrived to "liberate" the island for the first time. Except for a short period in the middle 1700's, when they were ruled by England, the Cubans had Spanish masters for four centuries. Rich from tobacco and sugar, the little island was also the target for continuing pirate raids in the 1600's and the 1700's.

The same urge for independence that set off revolutions throughout Latin America stirred the Cubans, but their geographic position prevented them from joining the successful ousters of the Spaniards that were taking place in the rest of Latin America in the early 1800's. Separated from their spiritual brothers and exposed more than anyone else to Spanish military might, the Cubans suffered foreign domination from Europe a half century longer.

Meanwhile, the Negro slaves that had first been imported in 1526 now outnumbered the whites, and the battle for freedom acquired the additional heat of a war for the end of slavery. In 1823, open revolution erupted and was quelled. In retaliation, Spain gave Captain General Vives absolute powers, which he promptly put to use by creating Cuba's first martyrs to independence. Four years later, as the result of a Negro uprising, more martyrs were made, including the poet Gabriel de la Concepción Valdes.

In 1847, under tremendous public pressure, slavery was officially abolished. But in practice, it continued, and not for another three decades were the Negroes really free.

In 1848 the United States offered Spain $100 million for Cuba—the South wanted the island for slavery. But the offer was turned down—twice—and Cuba remained under Spanish rule. The South kept hoping we would take over the island; in fact, in the Ostend Manifesto, it went so far as to declare Cuba ours by some sort of "natural right."

Another poet sought martyrdom in 1895, and found it in battle, to become Cuba's national hero: José Martí. Now, having failed to buy the island, the United States declared itself in sympathy with the rebels, and when the battleship *Maine* was blown up in Havana harbor in 1898, it served as the pretext for our declaring war on Spain. In December of that year, vanquished Spain yielded the island. To the Cubans? No: to the United States.

The United States established a provisional military government in Cuba in 1898 and did not turn the island over to the Cubans for four years. Meanwhile, U.S. business interests had bought, at war-depressed prices, $50 million worth of Cuban sugar and tobacco land, iron, nickel, and manganese mines. When the Cubans finally inherited in 1902 the land they had lost in 1511 they found a good part of its riches under foreign control.

They also discovered that the United States had passed the Platt Amendment which entitled us to intervene in Cuban affairs "if Cuban independence is threatened," and which gave us the right to lease naval and coaling bases on the island, including the Guantánamo Bay base which is so much in the news today.

United States troops landed in Cuba in 1906, 1912, and 1920; all this time Cubans smarted under the outrage of "limited independence." But the Platt Amendment was not abrogated until 1934, and then our right to Guantánamo was continued.

From 1925 to 1933, Strong Man Machado ruled the island —and our diplomatic representatives played "footsie" with him. He was overthrown by General Batista, under whom Cubans suffered even greater suppression than ever—and we awarded Batista medals and encomiums as a leader even as his government became more dictatorial and more corrupt.

Under Batista, gambling, prostitution, and various more subtle forms of vice were tolerated—for a rakeoff. Often, that rakeoff came from Chicago and New York racketeers, North American overlords of Cuban crime. And the patrons of the gambling casinos, elegant brothels, pornographic movies, and "circuses" were often North Americans, too, out of the country on vacation, their inhibitions left behind.

More important, under Batista some 20,000 Cubans were killed and countless others jailed and tortured. The weapons that he used came from us; so did the training his "army" received. All on the basis of "hemispheric defense," although the Cuban army hasn't fought a real war in this century.

As if this weren't enough, our official domination of Cuba after the Spaniards were ousted produced, in addition to the Platt Amendment, a curse disguised as a blessing—the sugar quota. We granted Cubans a handsome import preference on their sugar; in other words, we would buy their principal product at more than it was worth. Forget that our motivation was the protection of the price of sugar beets back home—for the Cuban, the offer was a bonanza. So cane was planted, and more cane, and we bought it. With the result that other crops disappeared: sugar was king. The island, with a climate and fertile soil suited to agriculture of all kinds like no other in the world, was soon forced to import foodstuffs. A third, then a half, of the food Cubans ate came from the United States. So did their manufactured goods since they were too busy making sugar to make much of anything else.

Year after year, the balance of payments between Cuba and the United States became more unfavorable to Cuba; as a nation and as individuals the Cubans owed us money. We granted more credit and the dance went on. The United States was Cuba's single buyer, its single seller, and nearly its single creditor. Cuba and the Cubans were our bonded slaves—this, after the sacrifices of men like José Martí (who had written, prophetically, "A country that trades only with one country dies").

This is what Cubans revolted against in 1959, when Fidel Castro and his *barbudos* came out of the hills. In the beginning, the Cuban revolution was a middle-class revolution, led by

29

doctors and lawyers and small businessmen and intellectuals who knew enough of the economic facts of life to recognize that U.S. domination was the real oppressor—and enough social psychology to know that Batista had to be the symbol against which their revolution was aimed.

These middle-class men, these intellectuals, have been betrayed by their own revolutionary leaders; their fight against economic domination has been resolved only by accepting the total domination of communism. Now they are fleeing to the States for asylum.

But we make a miserably foolish error if we read this flight as approval of our past policies in Cuba, of our early military domination, our later economic domination, and our continuing complicity with the dictators under whom Cubans have suffered. Cuba revolted as much, or more, against us as against Batista; the fact that it later fell to the Communists does *not* mean that any feeling against the United States must necessarily be, not the result of our own errors but of Communist agitation.

Just as there was, quite apart from the Communists, anti-Yanqui sentiment in Cuba, there is, quite apart from the Communists, strong feeling against us all over Latin America—even now, after the launching of the $20 billion Alliance for Progress.

Part of the reason lies in past policy failures on our part; the remainder in our past and present behavior as a nation and as individuals. Let's review the policy failures here, and go on to procedural errors in the several chapters that follow.

In 1826 Simón Bolívar called for the First American Congress, to organize friendly feelings among the Western Hemisphere nations and to protect them from outside attack. Our Congress debated for some five months whether to send delegates; when the vote was taken, and resulted in favor of so doing, it was too late for those delegates to arrive at the meeting. Held in Panama in 1826, the meeting failed—largely because of lack of backing from the United States.

Some 14 years later, in 1840, we developed the egotistic idea that we were in some way predestined to overspread the entire

Western Hemisphere, expressing that concept in the paranoic motto of "manifest destiny." It was on this basis that we went to war with Mexico in 1846; as the result of that war Mexico lost to us nearly half of its total territory. But even more important in a global sense was the result in terms of United States-Latin American relations: suspicion and fear of the "giant to the north" was germinated, and the American community was divided between the aggressive "haves" and the oppressed "have-nots."

In 1847 the Second American Congress met in Lima, Peru, to discuss the threat of Spanish reinvasion of South America. The United States, engaged in an aggressive war with Mexico, could not and did not send good will emissaries. When the Third American Congress was convened in Santiago, Chile, in 1856 to draft a "great American family" treaty, the United States was not even invited: fear and suspicion of us on the part of Latin Americans was already firmly established.

The Fourth American Congress met in 1864 in Lima to discuss the European menace to American peace and security represented by French support of Emperor Maximilian in Mexico, and Spanish seizure of Santo Domingo (now the Dominican Republic). The United States, involved in its own Civil War, did not attend.

In 1866, with the War Betweeen the States over, U.S. battleships were cruising once more. Some were in the Chilean port of Valparaíso—and were notified by Spain that that nation's ships were about to bombard the unprotected port. Although the Monroe Doctrine had been firmly enunciated 43 years before, we did not help the South American navies resist this invasion. Instead, our battleships weighed anchor and put to sea, leaving our neighbors, whom we had said we would defend, to their own devices.

Not until Latin America became commercially important to us did we manifest any real interest in the area and then only in an exploitative sense. With the rapid development of our industry after the Civil War, we began to look for new

31

markets—and fastened on Latin America. At this point only 15 per cent of our foreign trade was conducted with them, the balance of trade being distinctly unfavorable to us.

It was within this expansionist framework that we called the first Pan-American Congress in Washington in 1889. Although many salient issues were discussed, including a Pan-American railroad, bank, and customs union, nothing solid developed from the Congress, largely because of fear of the United States.

Then came the Spanish-American War, our occupation of Cuba, and the infamous Platt Amendment which we forced on Cuba and which forced on us the label of "Yanqui imperialists."

Then, in 1903, President Theodore Roosevelt reinterpreted the Monroe Doctrine as a mandate to intervene in Latin American affairs at will, and the era of the Big Stick was underway. In that same year the Colombian Senate rejected the Hay-Herrán treaty under which the United States was to acquire all rights to build and maintain a canal across the Isthmus of Panama, then a part of Colombia. It was on November 3 of that year that Panama revolted against Colombia—with U.S. armed forces standing by to see that the revolt would not be put down—and declared itself a separate republic. Three days later the United States formally recognized the new republic—and the Panama Canal was ours.

In 1906, in Rio de Janeiro, Secretary of State Elihu Root made a famous and much-loved-by-Latins speech calling Latin America our "elder sister" and declaring the United States firmly sensitive to the independence of all American nations.

The next year Secretary Root called the Central American nations to Washington to chastise them for constant bickering and fighting among themselves and to push them toward peace and unity. One of the most significant results of that conference was the founding of a Central American court of justice in San José, Costa Rica. We also pledged our moral support to the rulings of this court. Did this achievement offset the Big Brother air of our calling the meeting in Washington in the first place? Later events would answer that question. . . .

32

In 1915 U.S. Marines landed in the Dominican Republic and in Haiti, and stayed there maintaining order (and protecting our investments) until 1924 and 1934, respectively. In 1911 Marines landed in Nicaragua staying on until 1932. While they were occupying the latter country, we negotiated a treaty with Nicaragua which gave us an option on construction of another Atlantic-Pacific canal (through Lake Nicaragua) and rights to naval bases at both ends. This "Bryan-Chamorro Treaty" was considered null and void by the Nicaraguan public—but, under President Chamorro—a dictator backed up by North American bayonets—they could do nothing.

In their interests the governments of El Salvador and Costa Rica questioned the validity of the treaty in the Central American court of justice. The court ruled against the treaty, but Chamorro's government refused to recognize the court's authority. And our government, pledged to back up the court, maintained a profound silence.

In like manner each of the lofty pronouncements of the 1907 Washington meeting on Central American unity came to nought —largely because of the recalcitrance of Nicaragua, a country which we dominated financially, militarily, and politically.[3]

Four more Pan-American Congresses met, achieving a certain solidarity among the Latin American nations, but not between these nations and the United States. Then came the 1923 Santiago Conference which was divided at the outset by the fact that Latin America had enthusiastically joined the League of Nations, while the United States had not. But this rift was

[3] Nicaraguan Salvador Mendieta, founder of the Central American Unity Party, writes: "Before 1910, the institutions and the people of the United States inspired sympathy; but when we saw U.S. government agents descend to the lowest levels of political and economic morality, to exploit a generous country like Nicaragua without mercy and to debase our dictators with false promises, it produced a great shock to the Nicaraguan conscience; and later, Nicaraguans fell into complete lack of confidence in the purity of North American institutions, the faith of North American leaders, and the honor of the North American public." (*Alrededor del Problema Unionista Centroamericano: 1.* Editorial Maucci, Barcelona, 1934.)

as nothing compared to the announcement by our delegation that the Monroe Doctrine was a unilateral document to be interpreted only by the United States—followed by the return of our previously withdrawn Marines to Nicaragua, and the classic statement by President Coolidge that wherever there was a U.S. citizen or U.S. property, there was a little piece of the United States!

Through the Havana Conference of 1928 we wielded our Big Stick—and contributed to disunion among the Latin American nations and firm hatred for the United States. But in 1929 came "the crash" and a new posture of humility on our part. It was as a result of our national fear—a far cry indeed from the egoism of "manifest destiny"—that Franklin D. Roosevelt dedicated the United States to "the policy of the good neighbor."

Since that time, relations between the United States and Latin America have improved, although not at a rate commensurate with our policy improvement. A long history of injustice cannot be lived down by a few years of decent behavior, of course. But even more important, our policy changes have not been reflected by a change in the behavior of our personnel here—and, as usual, they have not been as deep-running as the fine words might make one believe. In the several chapters that follow, I will try to show exactly why.

3

Deaf and Dumb Diplomats

One hundred miles north of the Honduran coastline, all but lost in the vast blue Caribbean, lie two unimposing sand specks known as the Swan Islands. They are, depending on one's point of view, either "the U.S. only disputed territory" or "the islands the Yanquis stole."

They are also a symbol of continuing United States fumbling in this area, a stumbling block to the success of the Alliance for Progress, and a source of aid and comfort to the Communists in their plan to capture all of Central America.

Legally, the Swan Islands may well belong to the United States. But our claim, however technically correct, has helped our enemies so well that Honduran President Ramón Villeda Morales publicly declares his government's inability to stem the tide of Red infiltration. They are tiny, these little strips of beach surrounded by so much water, but they are far from insignificant.

Little Swan, no more than a mile and a half long and a half mile wide, is uninhabited. Great Swan, not much bigger despite its name, has had a sprinkling of inhabitants, most of them North Americans, since the late 1850's. That was when a U.S. citizen, George W. White, landed there and took possession in the name of the United States. Prior to that time (April 3, 1857) there seems to have existed no documentary claims of ownership on anybody's part.

In 1921, however, the Honduran Government declared that it owned the Swan Islands. Two years later in a note to the U.S. legation in Tegucigalpa, it based its claim on the assertion that the Spaniards had discovered the islands early in the 16th century. They contended that Spain's title passed to Central America by virtue of the latter's emancipation, and that in 1839 when the United Provinces of Central America dissolved, sovereignty over the Swan Islands passed exclusively to Honduras. However, neither the Honduran Government nor anyone else has presented any solid evidence that Spain discovered or possessed the islands in the first place. On this basis, the United States has maintained its claim and there the matter has rested for four decades, with little contention beyond the formal exchange of diplomatic notes.

But in March 1960, when the United States took a census of the islands, the Honduran press and public exploded. Under none-too-subtle but all too effective Communist prodding, every nationalistic Honduran (and it's hard to find any who aren't) joined Castro and the Reds in their tirades against U.S. "aggression."

University student leaders, traditionally Latin America's most politically volatile group, leaped to the defense of "national sovereignty," demanding that an expeditionary force be sent to the islands to take possession in the name of the Honduran people.

Capital daily *El Cronista,* the unofficial voice of communism in Honduras, immediately launched a campaign against this "territorial conquest" on the part of the United States. *El Día,* the nation's leading paper, almost always on the other side of the fence, this time agreed with its left-wing counterpart and censured the United States for having violated Honduran sovereignty.

North American interests had always exploited what little the islands had to offer—guano and coconuts—and there had been a U.S. Weather Bureau station on Great Swan since 1914, all without notable reaction from the Honduran public. But now, alerted by the Communists, this public rose to a fever pitch of indignation. The legal aspects were unimportant: what mattered was public sentiment. As usual, this proved to be an

36

instrument we ignored, while the Communists played on it like grand masters.

Instead of announcing immediately that we were willing to discuss the matter of sovereignty over the Swan Islands, we ignored the furor and went on to grant permission to a New York holding company, The Gibraltar Shipping Co., to establish a station there. (I cannot prove the truth or falsity of this, but it has been reported here and in the States that this "commercial station" is a front for our Central Intelligence Agency. It is true that "Radio Swan," now known as "Radio America," concerns itself largely with anti-Castro material prepared by Cuban exiles.) As a natural result, Castro and the Communists launched an all-out effort to eliminate this threat. Equally naturally, they appealed not to reason or to law, but to Honduran nationalism.

El Cronista intensified its anti-U.S. clamor, calling the Swan Island affair "cold, calculated, brutally unjust," and claiming that "in Honduras, there are no anti-American sentiments. What is proven is that the U.S. government has an incomprehensible hostility toward Honduras."

Dr. Villeda Morales' government, privately not too excited about the Swan Islands, was forced by public sentiment to take some action. In July 1960 it entered a formal protest to Washington, noting that the situation in the country called for early solution of the problem. But no answer was forthcoming.

So *El Cronista* turned its guns on the Villeda regime, accusing it of "sitting and waiting" for the U.S. answer instead of actively maintaining its sovereignty.

When the Organization of American States met in August 1960 in Costa Rica, Honduran Foreign Minister Andrés Alvarado Puerto put the matter to Christian Herter, then U.S. Secretary of State. Concerned with other, seemingly much more important matters, Herter said that the United States was not prepared to undertake a detailed examination on the spot, but that we would discuss the matter in Washington "in the near future."

37

Meanwhile, the issue became Latin American in scope. The "First Latin American Youth Congress," meeting in Havana, unanimously condemned the United States for its behavior in the Swan Islands and criticized Villeda's government for "manifest indifference" in the face of a violation of national sovereignty.

And Fidel Castro took advantage of the issue to denounce the United States in the U.N. General Assembly.

Then, when Herter told the OAS that Cuba was a menace to the rest of Latin America, *El Cronista* was able to counter by pointing to the Swan Islands, slyly asking, "Who is the real threat?"

Not until September 2, 1960 did Hondurans learn of the answer to their government from Washington. That answer stoutly maintained that the Swan Islands legally belong to the United States. It allowed that the State Department would discuss the matter if a Honduran delegation would take its case to Washington. In short, nothing had changed since Secretary Herter and Foreign Minister Alvarado Puerto had talked in San José.

The Federation of University Students, which had recently voted out its Red-lining directors by a narrow margin, responded to this stimulus with a new wave of nationalism and anti-Yanqui protest. The students demanded that the government occupy the Swan Islands, militarily and civilly, before Independence Day (September 15)—or else the students would invite the public to celebrate a National Day of Mourning.

President Villeda firmly informed the students that he and not they would determine the country's foreign policy—and then nipped their chauvinistic scheme in the bud by announcing on the 15th that he had sent another note to Washington. That note, he said, reported his willingness to discuss, "Not Honduras' sovereignty over a part of its insular territory, but the position of the United States in respect to the Swan Islands." (Privately, Villeda may feel less strongly about the matter. His personal friend and national chairman of the incumbent Liberal Party, José Mejía Arellano, recently told me: "It's a matter of

38

prestige: if the U.S. offered us a dollar a year for the use of the islands we could let them go ahead without losing face—and without arousing our people to the dangerous pitch they are at now. The U.S. doesn't seem to realize the problems of a small and poor country like ours. Here everything the U.S. does is viewed with suspicion, because it is so big and powerful and because it did dominate all of Central America until not too long ago. And every act of a local government is viewed against that setting. It's not easy to be friends with the United States.")

To date, the Swan Islands affair remains unresolved. Meanwhile, playing on the wounded dignity of the Honduran man-in-the-street, the Communists have become ever more active here, turning the country into the nerve center from which the intended Central American coup is being directed, as we shall see in Chapter 8.

Yet when I queried our Embassy in Tegucigalpa about the Swan Islands, its counselor, answering for the Ambassador, assured me that "only agitators present this as the 'perpetration of a violation of sovereignty,' " and explained that Honduras and the United States have agreed to discuss the matter—as if that settled everything.

He included a mimeographed statement that sets out the legal basis of the U.S. claim, but which has only this to say about the public relations implications:

"Sentiment in Honduras over this issue has grown to unprecedented heights over the past six months."

At the time of this writing, the Alliance for Progress has gone into effect and Honduras has applied for $11½ million on an emergency basis. But the cries of outrage over the Swan Islands are just as frequent, and louder, than the paeans of praise for our generosity. A costly bungle, for a nation that is desperately trying to win friends and influence people south of the border—and, latterly, that is putting its money where its mouth is.

The official explanation of the Swan Islands affair is that legally, they are ours. In like manner, when one or another of our ambassadors associates himself warmly and constantly with

39

a dictator, the answer is that legally, the dictator is the government, and one government must deal with another if it recognizes it at all.

Thus did we excuse the friendly relations between Ambassadors to Cuba Arthur Gardner and Earl E. T. Smith with Generalísimo Fulgencio Batista, to the continuing outrage of Cubans who suffered under Batista's long and bloody reign. And thus we excused the long-term personal friendship between Ambassador to Nicaragua Thomas Whelan and Dictator "Tacho" Somoza. Under a fairly rigid rotation plan, our Foreign Service representatives move from one country to another —but Mr. Whelan spent ten years in Nicaragua, trading drinks and meals with Somoza until Nicaraguans assassinated the latter.

Such behavior led to charges that the United States, for all its talk about democracy, is "soft" on dictators. Dr. Milton Eisenhower, commenting on that charge, said, "I am deeply disturbed by a gross misconception which is evidently fairly recent in origin. . . . Based on a distortion of facts, a false impression is now held by certain misinformed individuals and is also being cleverly fostered by communist agitators. . . . We are charged with supporting Latin American dictators."[1]

But in addition to the unhappy friendships just cited, there was what Salvador de Madariaga calls "the complaisant attitude of the Eisenhower Administration and of the President himself towards Somoza, Rojas Pinilla, Pérez Jiménez, Perón, and, last but not least, Franco and Trujillo.[2] . . ." During that administration, perhaps the most flagrant friendship was with the since-assassinated Dominican Republic dictator, Leonidas Trujillo, the self-appointed Generalísimo and Benefactor of his people. According to reports in our own press during Trujillo's reign, Mrs. Eisenhower's brother-in-law, Colonel Gordon Moore, paid several visits to Trujillo and, on one occasion, went into business with him on a sugar deal involving 7,000

[1] Op. cit.
[2] Salvador de Madariaga, "Challenge in Latin America: 1. Peoples and Politics," *Saturday Review*, March 25, 1961.

tons of cane; the late John Foster Dulles' son-in-law, during Mr. Dulles' tenure as Secretary of State, spent three months as Trujillo's guest in the Hotel Jaragua, having journeyed there in company with his wife and Mr. Dulles' grandchildren in Trujillo's personal plane. Henry Holland, Assistant Secretary of State for Latin American Affairs, quit his post and went to work for Trujillo to help him raise the U.S. quota on Dominican sugar. Numerous Congressmen enjoyed the Benefactor's hospitality, among them Donald Johnson of California and Garner Withrow of Wisconsin, who then returned to the States to sing the praises of the "democracy" in the Dominican Republic.

Several members of the House Committee on Agriculture and/or members of their families spent a pleasant all-expense-paid visit in Trujilloland in 1960, just before that committee voted to raise the Dominican sugar quota. Democrat John McCormack of Massachusetts, House majority leader, received the Order of Merit from Trujillo—and defended the Benefactor against all attacks thereafter.

Senator Allen J. Ellender, chairman of the Senate Agriculture Committee, also enjoyed Trujillo's hospitality, and returned to the States to eulogize him as "the sort of leader we need more of in Latin America." He was strongly backed by another Trujillo guest, Senator James O. Eastland, chairman of the Judiciary Committee.

And just to keep all the opprobrium from falling on the Eisenhower administration, a more popular name in Latin America found itself involved with the Dominican dictator when James Roosevelt, son of the implementer of the Good Neighbor Policy, was revealed to have been a representative for Trujillo in certain legal matters Stateside.

This foolishness, to give it the most complimentary label, does not exist only at the official level. During Trujillo's regime, any number of my compatriots here told me—and any Latins who would listen—that they liked the Dominican Republic better than any other Latin American country. As one put it, "It may be tough on them but it's sure good for us. Trujillo won't let a *dominicano* do a damn thing to an American!" They went on to explain that their suitcases and briefcases left in hotel rooms were always searched, but nothing was ever taken, so no harm was done. . . .

There are still too few Latin Americans who can read, but those who can, do—voraciously. The literate Latin is much more in touch with current events around the world than his North American counterpart. A person who reads only the U.S. press hears names and places mentioned in daily conversation here that are new and strange to him. And the nonliterate Latin follows events just as avidly over the radio, which is as big an attraction here as TV is Stateside. Thus our officials' and their families' dealings with people like the late Dominican dictator, and our citizens' preference for a country where they personally are safe, regardless of the condition of the local citizens, certainly does not pass unnoticed. I have before me, for example, the syndicated column of Roberto Garcia Peña, read widely in this part of the world, citing many of the facts I have just given. He treats them kindly, however, noting that people like Senators Ellender and Eastland are "more irresponsible than important."

But all these people are not directly concerned with United States-Latin American relations, and in any huge country such as ours it is difficult to co-ordinate the activities of experts in one field or of the general public with the activities of experts in other fields. Surely our representatives on the spot do better?

In my experience, they do not—except for rare cases.

I know of one Ambassador who, on meeting a local government official for the first time, asked him if he was a relative of the President. He was not, the man said. "Then," asked the Ambassador in evident surprise, "how did you get your job?" (There is still a great deal of what looks like nepotism in Latin America: the same family names keep cropping up in ministries, secretariats, and ambassadorships. This, of course, stems from the fact that few families in poor countries can afford to give their children the specialized education needed to become an effective Minister of Public Works or Attorney General—if

42

a President is to have an efficient Cabinet and supporting staff, he must choose from among a mere handful of families. The situation was quite similar when democracy was first being hammered out in the States: names such as Adams and Madison keep cropping up in our early history, and even such a democrat as Thomas Jefferson was accused of nepotism. In essence, nepotism as such exists only when competent people are bypassed to give jobs to incompetent family members and friends —what went on in the times of Adams and Madison and Jefferson, and what goes on in Latin America since the "hidden revolution" that replaced the dictators with democrats, is not really nepotism. And the parallel highlights once more that this area today is at the point the United States had achieved a century ago.)

An Embassy employee, who, after a state of siege had been in force two weeks in the country where he was serving, took a spin in the Embassy car after the curfew hour of nine at night. When signaled to stop by city police, he drove on—until shots from their carbines deflated his tires and created a needless international incident.

A vice consul who, at a consular party, made public remarks about "the natives and their barbarous language"—in front of several of "the natives."

Another vice consul who:

1. Replaced the popular director of the U.S. cultural center because she was a German, not a North American, causing vigorous student protest which he ignored. (Officially, the woman resigned—a "divorce of convenience," as it were.)

2. Demanded that students for course credit listen to Voice of America;

3. Established a conversational English course based on readings from *Time*'s Latin American edition, whose negative attitude toward much of Latin America we will examine in Chapter 5;

4. Called a popular local businessman "a dog thief and an ex-Nazi" when a watchdog lent him by this man doggishly ran home;

5. Earned the local nickname of "The Ugly American"[3]—and a promotion to a major European capital.

All of these men spoke only the poorest of Spanish and associated with local people only on the official level; all of them manifested a daily tactlessness that is the very antithesis of diplomacy. (It is significant that all of them operated in a country where our press representation is all but nonexistent, which allowed their behavior to remain unreported. Perhaps the greatest strength of our government system is the "checks and balances" arrangement, under which the performance of each branch is scrutinized by the others. But our diplomats overseas have no on-the-spot checks or balances except the press: where that safeguard is lacking, as it is in much of Latin America, errors can be and are repeated again and again.)

Association with local people solely on an official level seems to be a natural tendency of diplomats, those of other countries as well as ours. But especially in Latin America it is a lamentable tendency for a number of reasons. First among these is that the average Latin is the humble Latin—and his leaders, even when freely elected, do not really represent him in the sense of being like him. As a result of this factor and of the historical association here between government and oppression, the dominant emotional note of the humble Latin is anti-official: not yet fully adapted to emerging democracy, he tends to distrust even the leaders he helped install. Secondly, the Communists know and use this anti-officialism; their representation here, and in the majority of countries where they do not have embassies, is through Cubans—Latins "just like us" who talk to the poor in their *cantinas* and *truchas,* and in readily acceptable anti-government terms.

When our representatives confine themselves to the white tie and tails, champagne and caviar world, they establish a contrast with the behavior of these Communist representatives that breaks down the image of our much-vaunted folksiness and creates a picture of North Americans as rich, proud, and un-

[3] The people who called him this may not have read the book, but they much enjoyed the title.

caring. There are natural excuses for this: that the primary job of the diplomat is to deal with the local government; that the day-to-day burden of visa-stamping and press release-writing allows no time for jaunts into the hills; that transportation is often so poor that one can't get around outside the major cities. But in Latin America, local government still is subject to change without notice, and exclusive identification with it is shortsighted at best. If paper work ties down our diplomats, let's hire local, bilingual clerks and free the diplomats for real diplomacy. And if the roads don't suffice for our Lincolns and Cadillacs, let's get a horse.

Fortunately there are men who do just this. One of them is Ambassador to Costa Rica Raymond L. Telles, a man who is as popular in that country as its own President, and just about as much photographed and interviewed by the *tico* press. Ambassador Telles spends much of his time in the coffee farms and banana farms, in university and high school "bull sessions," and in union meetings. He holds a press conference twice a week—and talks straight from the shoulder, even if there is danger of speaking "against the book." Why? Because, as he says, "The Communists don't work at cocktail parties. One finds them with the workers. If we are going to give them a real answer, we have to go where they go. . . ."

Indeed, we must. But, with rare exceptions, we don't go there.

One reason for this failure is that most of our representatives here speak only the most rudimentary Spanish. This indicates a fundamental weakness in our Foreign Service training program that must be repaired before we can begin to hope for decent relations with Latin America. (There is, in the States, a certain disrespect for all languages other than English; I have often noticed that although every Ph.D. has passed a language examination in order to earn his degree, few indeed actually possess skill in the language in question: the requirement, in practice, is a mere formality. In like manner, perhaps our diplomats have passed language examinations—but they usually don't speak the language.)

It also seems that the rotation schedule under which officers are shifted from one post to another (as often as biennially) should be reviewed; and in cases where a man is serving well and happily, it should be ignored. I remember a political officer I met in Mexico who had married a Latin girl, brought his children up bilingually, and fit into the life of the community like a native. After less than three years he was transferred to Washington, despite his formal request to be left where he was. On the other hand, Tacho Somoza's friend, Ambassador Whelan, was left in his Managua post for ten years, indicating that the formula can indeed be ignored when State chooses to ignore it.

Similarly, the selection standards of the Foreign Service include the demand that an applicant be prepared to serve anywhere in the world. Thus, an enthusiastically pro-Latin North American who knows the area and the language will not be considered for employment if he specifies that he wishes to serve in Latin America!

But if the image of the United States projected by our diplomats here is unfortunate, equally so is the image of Latin America they relay home in reports and dispatches. Based on what the leaders tell them, they declare that we are well loved; that our policies are appreciated; that our people are welcomed, that communism is no real threat (who would expect Uncle Sam to give millions to a country about to go the way of Cuba?); that conditions are stable. As a result of this rosy view, we perpetuate policies and procedures that are getting us into trouble, and continue to offend our neighbors.

In an article in *Harper's,* I reported that Fidel Castro was still highly popular in Central America and that there was, as ever, resentment against our fruit companies. Replying to this article, one diplomatic official with 32 years of service, most of it in Latin America, declared that if either statement was true, he was certainly not aware of it.

Another diplomatic official declared that the article overstated the case as to anti-Yanqui feeling. "Very few Latins dislike us," he confidently asserted. But when asked how many Latins he

46

had talked with since his recent arrival in the area, he admitted that he had contacted almost none—his Spanish was too poor.

There is only one way to know what is going on in a country: go and see. There is only one way to know what a man thinks and feels: talk with him. Until our official representatives in Latin America do this, we will continue to misunderstand the area—and we will continue to be warmly disliked.

4

Blind Businessmen

Imagine a southern Indiana farmer in a year of drought looking for a job with the coal mines and being told that he can't be a timekeeper or a foreman because he doesn't speak Spanish. Or a Colorado householder receiving his light bill with quaint grammatical errors put there by the Latin American owners of Boulder Dam. Or a Texan told that Texas oil belongs to Venezuela.

These may be imaginary and laughable situations for us, but for the Latin American they are daily reality. As Peter F. Drucker reported in *Harper's*,[1] Latin Americans "are particularly sensitive about foreign ownership of their oil, electric utilities, telephone systems and railroads." I would extend his "oil" to any of the built-in riches of the soil and subsoil, whether oil or gold and silver and copper or bananas or coffee. Naturally. This is their land, and what comes from it or from beneath it, belongs by rights to them. The way a Texan feels about Texas oil or a Hoosier about his hybrid corn.

Nearly half of the 50 leading industrial firms in Latin America are U.S. owned and controlled, bearing names like Creole, Philips, Shell, Mobil, Sinclair, Texas Petroleum, and Celanese. The two largest, in terms of sales, are Creole and Shell of Venezuela; both North American companies, both in oil. The sixth and seventh largest belong to us, too, and they are oil companies. The tenth largest is ours: a mining company in Peru. In fact, among the dominant industries that belong to us in Latin America, almost all are engaged in the pursuits that

[1] "A Plan for Revolution in Latin America," *Harper's*, July 1961.

48

Latins feel they themselves should control—the ripping of riches from beneath the soil.

When we hear of complaints against us in these parts, we often cite in return the statistics of U.S. capital in Latin America —"development capital," we call it. But according to the Survey of Current Business, of our $8,365 million investment here as of mid-1961 $2,882 million was in oil; $1,155 million was in mining and smelting; $1,131 million was in public utilities.

In other words, well over half of our investments are in the very fields where our activity is specifically resented.

These are, of course, extractive industries, industries that wrench something out of the soil or subsoil and ship it elsewhere; industries whose incomes depend not only on cheap local labor but also on vigorous exploitation of cheap local natural resources. Quite apart from the Communist line, is it any wonder that we are known here as "exploiters"?

Granted that any foreign company engaged in an extractive effort faces huge public relations problems, one would automatically expect the nation that gave birth to Madison Avenue to mobilize its propaganda resources to counter the inherent difficulties. Among such resources would logically fall the use of a Spanish rather than an English corporate name; the employment of Latin Americans as directors and senior officers; the offering, at attractive rates, of corporate stock to local investors; the integration of North American personnel into the local community. In short, the greatest possible local identification and image should be the goal.

With rare exceptions, we do the exact opposite.

In 1955, the late Professor Richard B. McCornack of Dartmouth studied four large North American companies in Latin America. Three had names in English: United Fruit Company (some of whose subsidiaries have Spanish names, some not); the Braden Copper Co. of Chile; and Creole Petroleum of Venezuela. The fourth, Cerro de Pasco corporation of Peru, uses a Spanish name.

The president of Braden Copper is usually a Chilean; Creole has, as of this writing, four Venezuelans on its board of directors; officers of the other companies are usually North Americans.

Professor McCornack did not report on stock offerings, and I am unaware of the policies on this point of Braden and Cerro de Pasco. Creole's stock is marketed on the Caracas Exchange; United Fruit's only on the New York Exchange and is not in any way made attractive to Latin Americans.

Each of the companies Professor McCornack studied maintained company towns, although Creole was then attempting to integrate its North American personnel into the local community in a program that is still underway and much stressed by management.

Apart from this study, International Telephone and Telegraph made no effort to invite local ownership through stock participation. It was run out of Argentina and Cuba. American Foreign Power has lost several of its Latin American holdings; it, too, made no attempt to attract local ownership. Yet the U.S. Information Agency has reported that Latins who are against straight U.S. investment in their countries almost uniformly favor mixed investment, even when local control of the firm is only partial.

The examples of ITT and American Foreign Power were cited by Thomas Aitken, Jr., McCann-Erickson General Manager in Argentina, who believes that local stock participation is the real key to acceptance of U.S. investment in Latin America.

Mr. Aitken[2] also puts his finger on another sore spot of U.S. business here—the "dollar payroll" for North Americans and the much lower "local payroll" for citizens of the country in which the firm operates who do the same jobs. (And, sometimes, do them better.)

In like manner, John C. Shearer,[3] after studying how 23 U.S. firms utilize high-level manpower in Brazil and in Mexico, raises serious doubts about the nearly uniform policy of relying on

[2] "The Double Image of American Business Abroad," *Harper's*, 1961.

[3] *High-Level Manpower in Overseas Subsidiaries*, Princeton University Press, 1961.

transplanted North Americans rather than available local manpower, on the basis of cost as well as of the frictions created by this policy. He concludes that the development of management personnel in many of our Brazilian and Mexican ventures leaves a great deal to be desired.

My own primary experience is in Central America, and here the picture painted by Professor McCornack in Chile, Venezuela, and Peru, Mr. Aitken in Argentina, and Mr. Shearer in Brazil and Mexico is more than confirmed. It is also clearer and easier to study since one company is the dominant force in Central America. That company is United Fruit of Boston. Let's examine its performance in Central America, and especially in Honduras, where one need only say *"la compañía"* to indicate United Fruit.

Throughout Central America, UFCo. has turned useless jungles and swamps into productive farms; has built homes, hospitals, schools, and clubs; has maintained vast health and sanitation programs, virtually eradicating malaria in its own areas. The company has also endowed and helped support the Central American School of Agriculture at Zamorano, Honduras; has consistently paid its workers more than any other rural workers in the country. In addition, the taxes and wages the company pays are larger than those of any other single unit in Central America; in Honduras, for example, UFCo. contributes almost one sixth of the gross national product.

The company maintains a vast collection of economic tropical crops at Lancetilla, in the same country; has sent out, free, literally millions of seedlings to spread new and better fruits, vegetables, and timber trees throughout the American tropics.

Yet there always has been, and there is today, tremendous feeling against the company throughout Latin America and especially in the several countries in which the company has operating divisions.

Why?

Part of the answer is sheer size—UFCo., operating in Honduras, Guatemala, Costa Rica, Panama, Colombia, Ecuador, and the Dominican Republic, is known as *el pulpo*, "The Octo-

51

pus." Another reason lies in its special contracts with the various governments, including huge concessions of land, implying foreign control of national resources (extractive industry again) and foreign interference in local politics.

In spite of this, operating policies and public relations efforts keyed to offsetting the image of bigness and foreignness might have made UFCo. a welcome partner. Instead, the company seems consistently to have pursued policies calculated to make it—and U.S. business in general—disliked.

Some of its subsidiaries, such as Honduras' Tela Railroad Co., bear English rather than Spanish names, reminding people constantly of their foreignness.

No attempt is made to attract local stock ownership; no director or *top* executive of the company is a Latin American. Local managers are all North Americans, as are most department heads and other executives. Instead of integrating its North American personnel into the local community, UFCo. maintains company towns. Housing and other perquisites, including the use of company vehicles, are a function of position —which means that the gringo *jefes* conspicuously have the best. As a direct result of this segregation many company people and especially the women, speak Spanish poorly or not at all, even after years of residence. This language barrier, plus the natural tendency of most people to socialize with others of similar status or position, is reflected in parties and other leisure activity—the Latin hosts feel shut out on their own home ground.

The company does nothing to discourage this effective apartheid; it maintains no orientation program for North American employees, does not demand Spanish language ability or teach the language (except in a few essential cases of men who will supervise farm workers speaking only Spanish), in no way rewards employees who adapt to the local environment and make friends for the company. Instead, UFCo. maintains an "American School" attended by all U.S. children and the children of some Latins—who are chastised for speaking one word of Spanish, "because we're teaching English here!"

52

As is common among U.S. companies abroad, there are two distinct payrolls, one for North Americans, the other for local people. It is not unusual for two people in comparable positions to draw salaries 50 to 100 per cent apart. I recall a case in which a North American chief clerk with 3 years' service was replaced in his $450 a month job by a local man with 5 years' service, at $300 a month.

Vacations for local employees depend on salary and seniority, ranging up to one month a year. United States vacations are *all* one month plus travel time and travel expense. Even weekend activities play up the difference; beach houses, boats, and lake lodges are assigned to "first class employees"—most of whom are North Americans.

With such policies in obvious operation, even the best public relations campaign could not sell the company to Latin Americans. But public relations efforts are almost nil—one man does the job in each country—and they are directly pegged to publicizing the huge taxes paid by the company (bigness again), while such truly salable efforts as the agricultural school and the botanical gardens in Honduras remain virtually unpublicized and, in the local consciousness, unconnected with UFCo.

Recently the company has given much proud publicity to a plan whereby the land it owns will be turned over to local people, who will raise the bananas. UFCo. will buy their product, ship, and market it, thereby "going into partnership" with the nationals in the countries where it operates. Labor leaders point out that the company will thus avoid most of its current legal obligations to provide various labor benefits and to maintain schools and hospitals. Government agronomists note that most of the land is now unsuitable for production of the market-favorite Gros Michel banana because of a soil fungus imported on planting material in years past. Other critics wonder why the company is not extending its "partnership plan" to its highly productive, low-cost producing zone on Panama's west coast.

Perhaps all of these critics are overly skeptical; the company's past history leads to skepticism. It is possible that long-overdue enlightenment is now striking UFCo., but it will take a long time to live down its past no matter how drastically changed the new policies may be.

Initially, the banana companies, including United Fruit, came to Latin America under land concessions from local governments granting them huge acreages in return for development efforts, such as the construction of much-needed railroads. In Honduras, for example, there was hope for an east-west rail link to encourage the Central American Federation; UFCo.'s subsidiary, Tela Railroad Co., was to provide that link in return for some 200,000 acres of rich banana land. Today, all of Honduras' 900 miles of railroad are within the banana zone; there is no east-west hookup, and Tegucigalpa remains one of the few national capitals in the world without rail communication.

The history goes beyond mere noncompliance with promises, however. In the early days of the banana trade, all our companies here were rough-and-tumble outfits, dickering with dictators for concessions, supporting revolutions against governments they couldn't deal with, reaping the rewards when those revolutions were successful. But then, Latin America was a rough-and-tumble place, and it could be that one had to act this way to make a dollar.

Perhaps the classic example was the revolution led by General Manuel Bonilla in Honduras to overthrow President Miguel Dávila. The revolution began in 1910 and finally succeeded in installing Bonilla as President in February 1912. The story was told in the March 1933 issue of *Fortune,* and retold in the National Planning Association's *United Fruit Company in Latin America,* a book that treats the company more gently than any other. According to that version, Samuel Zemurray, president of the Cuyamel Fruit Company (later bought by UFCo.; Zemurray later became UFCo. head), was wondering how he could obtain the government concessions he needed in Honduras. Meanwhile, President Dávila was negotiating with bankers in the States for a loan to save his government from bankruptcy. The loan was offered—if the U.S. bankers could name their own agent to control Honduran customs collections in order to assure that payments would be made. Among the concessions Zemurray sought were certain customs exemptions; if the loan went through, he might not secure them.

Meanwhile, General Bonilla, a former Honduran President living in exile in the States and eager to return to power, seized upon the unpopularity of the proposed collection scheme as his best opportunity, and upon Zemurray as his best possible ally. He sought Zemurray out, described his plan, and received a loan sufficient to purchase the yacht *Hornet,* formerly used by the U.S. Navy.

On Zemurray's own power launch, General Bonilla, two cohorts, and their arms and ammunition (also financed by Zemurray) were carried out to the *Hornet* and loaded aboard. Once landed in Honduras, the revolution started, ending with the ouster of Dávila and the installation of Bonilla as President. The loan agreement that Dávila had hastily signed was repudiated by the Honduran Congress; Zemurray was given every concession he sought.

Even this bare outline, indicating the meddling of our banking and banana interests in Honduran politics, up to and including the financing of a revolution, tells a sad historical story on the basis of which one can easily understand resentment in Honduras against Yanquis. Further facts are supplied by Lucas Paredes, noted Honduran journalist, in his book, *Drama Político de Honduras.* Paredes states that General Bonilla "compromised himself to give liberal concessions to the North American capital that financed his revolutionary adventure"; that he "handed over to concessionists the most valuable resources of the country"; that "the current economic chains we wear are owed (in part) to General Bonilla." Note that Paredes is an admirer of the General. He writes: "He was a great captain in war and, in peace, a lover of progress. As Chief of State he left his mark by giving tremendous impetus to primary education; he gave legislation of the most advanced sort. . . . As a

55

politician he committed great errors for which history cannot absolve him, but as a governor he left behind works that even time cannot destroy."[4]

Cuyamel is not UFCo., of course, although it later became part of "The Empire in Green and Gold." However, similar involvements in local revolutionary politics have been charged to United, including a 1915 border skirmish between Honduras and Guatemala and the more recent overthrow of Guatemalan Communist President Jacobo Arbenz. Arbenz had expropriated nearly 200,000 acres of UFCo. land; when he was ousted by Colonel Castillo Armas in 1954, all of this land was returned to the company.

As noted earlier, supporting revolutions and playing games with dictators may have been the only way to do business in Latin America up until, say, the end of World War II. But thereafter the area began to undergo what Adolf Berle has called a "hidden revolution" which is still not complete but which has replaced the old-style *caudillos* with freely elected democrats in all except a few countries. Since that revolution took hold, the old rough-and-tumble style of U.S. business here has not only won us the same fond hatred as before—it has also proved uneconomical.

In the ten years following the kickoff of the hidden revolution, UFCo.'s net income before taxes fell from $105½ million in 1950 to $20,887,760 in 1959. Earnings per share plunged steadily from $7.49 to $1.39. Value of the once blue-chip stock dropped from 73⅝ (in 1951) to 26 in 1959, and sank below 20 for the first time in recent history in 1960.

Company management blames this recent showing on such natural disasters as wind losses, plant diseases, and unfavorable markets. Perhaps a more likely explanation is that Ecuadorean bananas, produced at a cost of $2 a stem, are capturing the market, while UFCo.'s cost per stem is approximately $3.50. That high cost derives from the continuation in the new Latin America of policies and procedures developed in the old Latin

[4] Lucas Paredes, *Drama Político de Honduras,* Editora Latino-Americana, S.A., Mexico, 1959.

56

America, including the maintenance of company towns, railways, electric power systems, and, most of all, the policy of owning huge blocks of land, whether in production or not.

UFCo.'s Ecuadorean competitors face none of these costs—and none of the public and private frictions that accompany them. They buy, ship, and sell bananas. And they make a great deal of money, without making any enemies. Perhaps UFCo. might have done the same in the years since the hidden revolution started had its management recognized and adapted to the changed social and political climate in Latin America. Certainly it could have done no worse—showing an earnings decline of 15 per cent in a period when Standard & Poor's 50 industrials increased their average earnings 3½ times!

These criticisms, of course, do not apply to all U.S. business in Latin America, nor is feeling uniformly against such business when properly conducted. Sears, Roebuck & Company in Mexico and Brazil is well liked, and accepted on the same basis as any other local retail operation. As well it might be—Sears provides jobs for Latins and is a huge buyer of Latin-made products: fewer than 1 per cent of its employees are North Americans; less than 3 per cent of the merchandise it sells is imported. And it does not repatriate its profits: from the Brazilian operation it has removed only 1½ per cent per year on its investment.

Similarly, no Argentines are up in arms against Industrias Kaiser Argentina for the simple reason that the company is 51 per cent Argentine-owned, and employs only ½ per cent non-Argentine personnel!

It is not against firms such as these, with their enlightened policies and good public relations practices, that Latins rail when they talk of us as exploiters. Unfortunately, however, the friend-making of a Sears or a Kaiser is less widespread than the enemy-making of a United Fruit: the latter has nearly ten times as many employees as the two former put together, and operates in many more countries.

On the other hand, all the blame for UFCo.'s unpopularity cannot be laid to its policies: it is likely that no foreign firms engaged in extractive pursuits here could be warmly liked. (It is significant that our extractive interests here, which, as we have seen, comprise the bulk of our investment in Latin America, have generally been the poorest planners in social and political terms.) It seems to me that the gradual withdrawal of these interests, coupled with increased investment in nonextractive pursuits, is a first step in any program of aid to Latin America from which we hope to draw dividends in terms of amity. In Chapter 11 I will present a plan for this move. But first, let's turn to some other notable failures on our part to win friends and influence people in Latin America.

5

Nearsighted Newshounds

I have visited the States only a few times in the last several years, and each time for no more than a week or two. But every time I have been impressed by the startling lack of information the average North American has about this huge southern back yard of his.

On one trip, a clerk in one of the small New York shops wrote my address "Horundoo," and seemed surprised when I corrected it. A cabdriver commented that he was glad "they threw out that Trujillo in Cuba"; a businessman asked me how things were "down there in Honduras and Chile and the rest of South America."

But where are our people going to get their information? The great mass educator, of course, is the press. And in regard to Latin America our press is all but silent, even now, after the events in Cuba and the launching of the $20 billion Alliance for Progress. This silence is justified on the basis that "our readers don't care"; lacking daily information about the area, those readers have no reason to care.

Of course our press smeared the Cuban fiasco all over page one, but its handling of the story was, in the words of one N.Y. *Times* staffer of many years' experience, one of the worst jobs he had ever seen. The *Times* itself was blamed (by former Ambassador to Cuba E. T. Smith) for having run a series that "likened Castro to Abraham Lincoln" and made him "able to get followers and funds in Cuba and the U.S." During the attempted invasion of Cuba, our reporters told the world that "the Isle of Pines has fallen . . ." "the Cuban Navy has revolted

. . ." and that "rebel planes raid Havana." None of this was true, and the invasion attempt failed.

A large part of the difficulty lay in the fact that our reporters were attempting to cover, at a distance, an area with which they were not familiar. Before the Cuban Revolution, there was virtually no interest in Latin America on the part of our press, except for the latter days of Perón in Argentina, when we began to fear that Perónism would serve as a Western Hemisphere contagion point for Nazism. The number of full-fledged bureaus of our press in Latin America was, and is, pathetically small. For example, among the news magazines, *Time* has four, *Newsweek* has one, *U.S. News* has one. Few full-time correspondents cover Latin America, and these restrict themselves, in the main, to Mexico and Brazil. For the rest, our press gets its Latin American news from the wire services, whose representation here is also slight, and from stringers, only a very few of whom are professionally competent. The results of such inattention show up not only in embarrassing failures such as the Cuban invasion coverage, but also in events of lesser drama although perhaps equal significance such as those cited by British Reporter Henry Brandon in the *Saturday Review:*

"No American newspaper, so far as I know," Brandon writes, "had a staff correspondent in Guatemala during the attempted coup d'état last November. . . ." "There was no American staffer in Bolivia when a Soviet delegation from the Supreme Soviet visited that country last December. . . ." ". . . early in January a right-wing coup was forestalled in Venezuela; it received no mention in the American press"[1]

As another example, the full story of the Swan Islands, with which I began Chapter 3, has yet to be told in any newspaper or magazine Stateside. Perhaps this is because not one of our newspapers or magazines maintains a full-fledged bureau anywhere in Central America, and virtually none cover the area with a full-time correspondent. As a result, such face-costing

[1] Henry Brandon, "Challenge in Latin America: 2. Tasks for the Press," *Saturday Review,* March 25, 1961.

fumbles as that in the Swan Islands do not come to the attention of our public and are not emphasized sufficiently in Washington. In the absence of such emphasis, diplomats may and often do underrate crises or fail to report the unpleasant results of their own actions.

Again in Mr. Brandon's words, from the same article: "The American correspondent is an indefatigable digger for facts, a prodigious news and information gatherer. He has many more opportunities to talk to people than an ambassador, and in a sense he is a more disinterested person than the diplomat. Ambassadors who know that the country they are accredited to will remain unreported in the American press, may be tempted to cut corners in their own reporting. . . ."

I agree with Mr. Brandon that the U.S. correspondent is, or can be, a prodigious fact gatherer. But he can also be superficial, misled, and misleading. Recently I received, from worried relatives in New York, a clipping from "the good, gray" *Times*. Written by their Central American correspondent after a two-month swing through the area where I've been living for several years, it frightened my relatives with the headline, CENTRAL AMERICA FEARS INVASIONS, and the subhead, "Nearly All Nations in Region Suspect One Another." According to the story, for the past several months Central America had been kept on edge with varying degrees of invasion jitters; the writer's two months from Mexico to Panama had convinced him that each country feared the other was harboring invasion forces. Costa Rica was feared, the *Times* said, "because of mounting tension in the current Presidential campaign there." And Honduras had "fought off two invasion attempts in as many years."

But at the time this report appeared, relations among the Central American states were more amicable than at any previous time in history. Honduras and Nicaragua had peacefully settled a 60-year-old border dispute; the Central American cooperative bank had begun operations in Honduras; the Ministers of Economy had met to move toward a common market; the Ministers of Foreign Relations had begun a restructuring

61

and strengthening of the Organization of Central American States (including the formation of a new policy of mutual consultation before any republic makes a political move that might affect any other); the Ministers of Defense had discussed joint military action in the event of any external attack, especially by the Communists.

Furthermore, how can Costa Rica be feared, election campaign or no, when that peaceful nation has no army at all? And how can the two armed attacks made on the Honduran Government be described as "invasions" when they were led by a Honduran ex-army colonel at points far removed from the border?

Of course, the story in the *Times* conforms with the stereotype of Central America as a collection of unstable "banana republics" in which mutual invasion is as routine as baseball back home. But it misinforms its readers and insults the new and mature efforts of a gallant people struggling to achieve democracy, stability, and federation in the face of continuing Communist agitation and North American misunderstanding.

So far, we have been examining the effects of poor coverage of Latin America in the States. Perhaps even more significant, however, is the effect of that coverage here. Latins reading most of our publications feel like forgotten men, finding in the sparse coverage a sign of what a Brazilian paper once called "the underdeveloped policy of the U.S. in Latin America." And the one U.S. publication they see in which there is relative quantity leaves a good deal to be desired in the way of quality. That example is the Latin American edition of *Time* magazine —an edition that one of my Costa Rican friends once said would be better for U.S. prestige here were it not issued at all.

It is easy to see why. For example, in Honduras, after a stormy history of dictatorship, revolution, and more dictatorship, the people finally have a freely elected, genuinely democratic government. President Ramón Villeda Morales, a leading physician and ardent humanist, took office in December 1957. *Time*'s coverage of the events leading up to the election:

September 3, 1957—"Three years ago Honduran Liberal

Party Chief Dr. Ramón Villeda Morales, 48, nicknamed 'Little Bird,' had a badly busted wing. . . . Last week . . . he was riding high. . . .

"For the last eight months Villeda had been serving as Honduran Ambassador to Washington. *The stay in the U.S. apparently had done him good.* (Italics mine.) Washington received him warily, largely because of his leftist campaign oratory in 1954, e.g., promising *campesinos* an eight-hour day at double and triple pay." (U.S. workers have long had an eight-hour day—and triple the 1954 Honduran average is still only $1.50 a day, which many Hondurans are now getting, thanks to Villeda's having fulfilled the promise *Time* calls "leftist.")

The article concludes: "But Villeda Morales proved himself a much sobered man." This implies that the Honduran presidential candidate was a wild-eyed left winger, but saw the light after eight months in Washington—the home, apparently, of all right-thinking people. Not a pretty compliment to a probable chief of state, and not a pretty attitude for the Latin American edition of any U.S. publication.

October 7, 1957—"The little nation of Honduras was button-busting proud of itself last week. It had achieved what amounted to a near political miracle: a fair election. . . . Here and there a voter was crowned by a bottle of indelible ink (designed for staining index fingers to prevent double voting). Four people were killed in political fights—but this was less than the normal weekend toll from drunken machete brawls. The victors: the leftist Liberals, led by Pediatrician Ramón Villeda Morales. . . .

"Villeda had won the [Honduran presidential] election in 1954 on a *wild-eyed program* [*Italics mine*] promising double and triple wages to farmhands. . . . But eight months in Washington . . . had a sobering effect. . . . *He . . . announced that he was categorically opposed to Communism. . . .*" (*Italics mine.*)

Here we go one step farther, to the clear implication that Villeda had been pro-Communist; yet there is no record that he ever was, or that his U.S. stay had set him straight.

Time continues:

63

"The Assembly . . . can either name Villeda President or schedule elections, which he claims to prefer. . . ."

Why "claims"? This implies that Villeda is no democrat, and really wants the Presidency any way he can get it. But in 1957 he could have won any election, so why *not* prefer it?

Despite *Time,* Villeda became President. He went to work on health, welfare, education, and transportation for his country's nearly 2 million people. He built schools, health centers, roads, and bridges, gave workers a realistic labor code. *Time* reported not one word of this. Then he projected a hydroelectric plant on turbulent, unharnessed Río Lindo to help industrialization by increasing many-fold his nation's severely limited (22,000 kw) installed capacity. *Time* declared on October 20, 1958:

"The [World] Bank argued that roads are more important than a big dose of power for a primitive country, gave Honduras a $5 million highway loan, hoping to encourage a big road-building program. The effect was just the opposite."

It was not. In his first year in office, Villeda started building more miles of road than Honduras had previously had in its entire 139-year history. He is now building the Río Lindo hydroelectric plant as well, with $16 million loaned by banks, including the Import-Export bank, that agree that power is essential to the country's further development.

Note that *Time* used, and uses as often as possible throughout its Latin American coverage, the word "primitive" to describe Honduras. There are, of course, primitive areas in all of these countries, areas in which non-Spanish speaking Indians live in the shadow of ancient traditions. But as countries, now with modern air conditioned buildings, far-flung air transportation and, most important, democratic government, they are far from primitive, Honduras included.

Even on nonpolitical stories, *Time*'s deprecation of this struggling nation reveals itself. In March 1957 a boy drowned near Tegucigalpa. Then U.S. Ambassador Whiting Willauer, a skin diver by avocation and a nearby resident, was asked to retrieve the body, and did. *Time*'s report:

"Last March (Willauer) learned that being *the only pro-ficient skin-diver in the entire country* let him in for chores the State Department never visualized. . . ." (Italics mine) The fact is that Honduras' port of Tela, with one of the Caribbean's most beautiful white sand beaches, and the nearby Keys, are and long have been skin-divers' haunts, helping make the sport popular and its fans proficient. Former Ambassador Willauer could dive, but he was far from the country's only accomplished diver.

After minor stories in which it made sure to label Honduras as "primitive" once more, *Time* (January 11, 1960) published this classic:

Quoting *El Cronista,* capital daily, it described the country as suffering from "spiritual helplessness and a chronic economic depression." In the same story, with typical *Time* horror, it re-ported that "Communists are beginning to elbow their way into the nation's press." *Time* failed to note that *El Cronista,* the authority it quoted a few lines earlier, is the principal Com-munist-dominated paper in the country and has been fran-tically supporting, and receiving financial support from, Fidel Castro's revolutionary government.

Concluding the same story, *Time* declared: ". . . the longer he flutters, the less Little Bird looks like the stormy petrel he seemed before taking office."

But Villeda, in addition to his clear record of social accom-plishment, had meanwhile successfully handled a couple of armed attacks from the extreme right; replaced an entire re-calcitrant police force with a loyal Civil Guard; neatly coun-tered Communist agitation—all without declaring a "state of siege" such as neighboring Guatemala, Nicaragua, and El Sal-vador had found necessary. Furthermore, he avoided major strikes in the ailing banana industry, mainstay of the nation's economy, and he attracted major capital investment from abroad in a period when such investment was on the decline through-out most of Latin America (see Chapter 4).

Were *Time*'s self-conscious cuteness aimed only at Villeda, one might see it as an isolated prejudice—perhaps because

65

Honduras is, in *Time*'s words, "tiny and primitive." But this alleged news magazine, *read throughout Latin America as the voice of the United States,* maintains the same smug, belittling attitude toward virtually everything Latin American.

Items:

Paraguay (January 2, 1956)—". . . it is bad form in Latin America to plot just before Christmas. But last week, disregarding . . . all considerations of good taste, Strongman Stroessner's enemies tried to throw him out."

Brazil (January 16, 1956)—". . . foregoing his gimpy English, the President-elect talked to Ike in Portuguese, translated by . . ." (For that matter, what about Ike's nonexistent Portuguese?)

Nicaragua (October 1, 1956)—". . . portly, genial President Anastasio Somoza . . ." (was assassinated). "Gunman López Pérez . . . had left at least one clue that hinted at an obsession for martyrdom . . . his motive may well have been an itch for self-glorification." (Or could it have been that López Pérez didn't find thieving Dictator Somoza nearly as "genial" as did *Time?*)

Ecuador (Letter to the Editor, September 30, 1957, from Leonidas Plaza, Ecuadorean Ambassador in London)—*"Time* described my country as 'tiny and poverty-ridden.' Ecuador's area is equal to that of Great Britain or Italy and therefore cannot be described as tiny. Its national income is quite adequate for a young, underdeveloped country of 3,500,000 inhabitants. The difference between 'tiny and poverty-ridden' and 'relatively small and underdeveloped' . . . can make or break a commercial proposition or immigration plan."

Costa Rica (June 23, 1958)—Ex-President José Figueres, one of Latin America's most respected democrats and a friend of the United States, was asked to tell our House of Representatives why the United States is disliked south of the border. He did. *Time*'s report:

". . . outspoken Pepe so exaggerated and overstated his case that great pieces of his statement ended up sounding sadly like the *Yanqui*-baiting he deplores . . ."

66

Don Pepe is and was outspoken—that's why he was asked to give the talk in the first place—but there was little in his statement that was exaggerated or overstated, unless any criticism of the United States, even by invitation, must necessarily be so characterized.

Venezuela (July 21, 1958: *Time*'s first reference to Presidential Candidate Rómulo Betancourt, another leading liberal with pro-U.S. leanings)—"Key to the political puzzle was beefy Rómulo Betancourt, 50, top man of the leftist Democratic Action. . . . Betancourt now takes a carefully statesmanlike line."

Bolivia (March 2, 1959)—"Last week a U.S. embassy official added up the results [U.S. aid to Bolivia] and made a wry face. 'We don't have a damn thing to show for it,' he said. 'We're wasting money. The only solution to Bolivia's problems,' he went on to wisecrack, 'is to abolish Bolivia. Let her neighbors divide up the country and the problems.' "

Time's story enraged Bolivians, triggered anti-U.S. riots in which several people were hurt and significant property damage was done. On March 16, calling the story "The Fanned Spark," *Time* reported, "This rueful jest, repeated by a U.S. official in La Paz and quoted in *Time*'s March 2 issue, was turned last week into the spark for three days of anti-U.S. violence. . . . The U.S position was that there was 'no evidence' that the statement was ever made. . . ." In a footnote, *Time* sanctimoniously reported that U.S. readers had not seen the quote, which appeared only in the Latin American edition. Why, one wonders, did it have to appear at all? Admittedly, journalism is one thing and diplomacy another. But this fact does not excuse our press from all sense of responsibility, especially in a time of cold war as deadly as if there were shooting going on. And least of all does it excuse *Time,* which vaunts itself as the voice of much, if not all, of the United States, and which uses its pages as instruments of opinion-making even more than opinion-reporting.

Surveying the Latin American edition of *Time* over a four-year period (1956–1960) one finds a consistent tone of smug

67

superiority, a persistent flow of ridicule for many things Latin American. True, there are occasional favorable stories—but *Time*'s favors are rarely bestowed on any performance south of the border that doesn't neatly mirror life in the United States. Even then, the snide *Time* style intrudes: in a story commending Brazil, for instance, *Time* couldn't resist labeling its industrial explosion as "Johnny-come-lately industries." In general, any town smaller than Rio de Janeiro is described as "sleepy," any nation less developed industrially than, say, Mexico, as "backward" or "primitive," any politician other than a complete reactionary as "leftist," any plan for development as "starry-eyed," any appeal to the United States as "dollar hungry."

In some 200 issues of *Time*'s Latin American edition, fewer than half a dozen cover stories were about Latin America. In more than half of these issues, "Foreign News" ran ahead of "The Hemisphere"; in virtually every issue, quantity of Latin American coverage was substantially below that of news from outside the hemisphere. And, of course, every issue was printed in English rather than Spanish.

One wonders how such an edition can be called "Latin American"; one understands why my Costa Rican friend said it would be better for the United States if no such edition were printed. The rules of journalism should demand that *Time* restrict its deprecating tone to its domestic issue, and that its "Latin American" edition serve Latin Americans with unslanted, uncolored news.

It seems that *Time*'s wise-guy style has softened somewhat since about mid-1961. If this change proves to be permanent, we will no longer hear statements like this one by a Central American Cabinet minister:

"Magazines like *Time* prejudice Pan-American closeness, serving as a constant source of ill will toward the U.S."

I have analyzed *Time*'s coverage of Latin America in some detail because Latins do read it as "the voice of the U.S.," perhaps in part because it so represents itself. But its denigration of Latin America is not, unfortunately, unique. Take, for example, sister publication *Life,* which not too many years ago warned the North American public that "a single foolish action" could damage the United States "incalculably." Yet in its July 28, 1961 issue, *Life* carried an article, "Which Way Latin America?" by Robert Coughlan. It wasn't a bad article at all. But right in the beginning it showed its author's prejudice by describing Latin America thus:

"The massive illiteracy and poverty, the sweeping mismanagement, the racial and class animosities, the widespread resentment of the United States, the wild political factionalism, the appetite for intrigue and violence, for loot, for display, incongruously joined to a self-pity and eagerness to blame others —these things are not going to change overnight, and some of them not in this generation."

Apparently, *Reader's Digest* in no way disagreed with this sweeping, and inaccurate, condemnation of Latin America: it included the lines as written above in its condensation of the piece in November 1961, to the incalculable damage of United States popularity in these parts.

And then there was the case of *Vision,* written in Spanish for Latin American consumption, which published an article on the Pan-American highway with which one of its readers took issue. *Vision* failed either to print or to acknowledge his letter, although it was written on official stationery by a Minister of Public Works intimately involved with the planning of the Pan-Am highway!

As a Colombian journalist once chided me in Barranquilla: "Yes, you have a free press. But free for *what?*"

6

Inefficient Experts

Technical co-operation—the sharing of knowledge and skills with other countries—has a longer history in Latin America than anywhere else, and has covered a wider range of programs. Out of this vast, diverse effort has come a great deal of good, and a great deal of harm. In general, the good has been in terms of agricultural, educational, or health improvement for the host country; the harm has been in terms of the impression our experts have made on Latin Americans. These specialists, from mining engineers to missionaries, have impressed on Latins our proficiency in matters technical and our deficiency in matters human.

Some of the reasons for this were spelled out by the National Planning Association in its major study of technical co-operation in Latin America published in 1956. Abstracts from one report:

"Over and over, discussions of technical cooperation lead finally to this kind of remark: 'After all, success or failure . . . boils down to the quality of personnel.' This, we believe, is a true statement and, under present circumstances, a discouraging one. One of the most serious and continuing problems has been to find, train, and keep qualified technicians and administrators who will serve abroad. . . .

"This problem is not only recognized by those who have struggled with it in the successive U.S. agencies, but many Latin Americans have expressed their concern. They believe that much greater care should be exercised in selecting U.S. technicians. . . .

"Some of the qualities which a technical cooperation employee should have in addition to his technical experience and skills: He should be acquainted with and sympathetic to the traditions and culture of the host country and should speak the language of his hosts, understand the characteristics of the people and the organization of their government, know economic and social conditions in the host country, and have a flexible approach to methods through which development can be accelerated."

This, of course, is technical language, lacking emotional impact, to describe a human problem. But those of us who have lived here and seen our experts in action can testify to the emotional results of behavior that stems from ignorance on the one hand and arrogance on the other.

There is in one town where I have lived a farmer whose great success is the result of vast training and experience. Born in Greece and educated in Italy, where agricultural research is on a par with any in the world, he served as an adviser to the Marshall Plan in Greece, and later as a consultant to the Argentine and Honduran Governments. Now he has a model farm, raising fruits and vegetables whose scientific cultivation is excelled only by their mouth-watering appearance and flavor.

A visiting agricultural expert from the States had heard about this man and his farm, and asked me to introduce him and serve as interpreter. First we toured the farm, which visibly impressed the visiting expert. Then we went back to town to talk with the farmer.

The first question out of the visitor's mouth was, "Why don't you try some of the ever-bearing varieties we grow in California?" The answer: They had been tried, but because of climatic differences between California and the tropics, had not done well. "Well, then, why don't you use such-and-such a fertilizer?" That, too, had been tried and found wanting. This sort of exchange went on for two hours, during which I found myself growing more and more ill at ease. Why couldn't the visiting expert recognize the expertise of the farmer he was interviewing? Why couldn't the conversation be an exchange of information

71

instead of a lecture in miniature? Why didn't the visitor ascertain, before presuming to give advice, that the local farmer's yield per acre was greater than the "standard" the visitor was bragging about back home, with quality at least as good?

Dr. Marston Bates, who spent many years in the tropics and loves the place as I do, wrote once: "I am always bothered by the Western arrogance, by its assurance that it knows all of the answers and can quite readily fix everything so that the tropical peoples will live happily ever after, if they will only listen. This philosophy underlies all of the various programs of international technical assistance that are so popular these days, and especially the programs of the United States which are aimed at the uplift of practically everybody else.

". . . [The] need for more knowledge about agriculture seems to me particularly striking because agricultural practises are intimately linked with the climate, and it is in climate, in the basic nature of the conditions of plant growth, that the tropics differ most from the north. I do not see how one can learn, in New York or Illinois or Kansas, to deal with the tropical environment; yet we quite confidently send our young experts from such places to Colombia and Siam to tell the 'natives' what they ought to do."[1]

Dr. Bates uses the word "arrogance," a word I avoided in an article about our behavior here, attributing it to fear, instead. I was brought to task for this avoidance by a fellow North American abroad, D. J. Cloward, director of the International School in San Pedro Sula, Honduras, former manager of the United Fruit Company division in this country and a man with some 42 years of tropical experience. Mr. Cloward wrote me:

"You question the possibility that citizens of our country are irrevocably arrogant. Their general actions and behavior when abroad would certainly negate your thought. . . .

"The fact that we actually have and are treating them as an inferior people in many instances is the chief basis for the ill

[1] Marston Bates, *Where Winter Never Comes*, Charles Scribner's Sons, New York, 1952.

will toward us that exists in these countries today. . . . We consider ourselves 'top dog' in the world of today, confident that our way of life is the right one, and full of zeal to help the less fortunate to convert to our system. In recent years swarms of purveyors of U.S. 'know-how' have descended on Latin America. Our diplomats have gone all out to influence these countries to copy our type of democracy, our bankers to show financial institutions how to imitate our fiscal setup, our military to train locals in modern soldiery, our missionaries to change habits and beliefs of worship, our labor experts to show local innocents how to organize unions and conduct strikes, our scientists, engineers, agriculturalists, educators and other specialists how to change ageless methods and customs even to eating and sleeping habits.

"People usually resent change even when it is for their own good; and in offering help and advice we do it with the unspoken but implied thought that these countries are at fault for their present conditions and should have imitated us long ago. This is irritating to the sensitive and proud Latin nature, particularly when it is advisable to meekly accept the advice in order to get a piece of the financial melon which is being handed out.

"While there is considerable 'window dressing' about cooperation between equal states in this melon distribution, the ordinary Latin who reads his newspapers knows that he and his country are considered backward and are being given a dole like a poor (and inferior) neighbor or relative . . ."

Time has passed since I wrote the article Mr. Cloward commented on, and I have seen more of our experts in action, serving as an interpreter for several of them. I have also followed the enunciation and launching of the Alliance for Progress, which I will examine in detail in a later chapter, and Latins' private reactions to this newest dole, with its demands that certain social, political, and economic conditions be fulfilled before the money will be forthcoming. I am forced to agree with Dr. Bates and Mr. Cloward: we are, almost uniformly, arrogant.

There are, fortunately, exceptions. The outstanding one is the Rockefeller Foundation, which operates agricultural aid programs in Mexico, Colombia, and Chile. I have heard vigorous praise of these programs from citizens of all three countries, and no criticism whatsoever.

Why?

First of all, no program starts until a host country invites Rockefeller co-operation. Then, the Rockefeller operation is organized as an integral part of the host country's Ministry of Agriculture; the Mexican office, for instance, is known as the "Oficina de Estudios Especiales" of the Ministry of Agriculture, carrying no foreign label whatsoever.

North Americans are employed, originally, to get the program moving. They are selected for high personal as well as scientific quality; they and their families must plan a career in international agriculture, not just "a job." They work from the start in close association with local scientists, who ultimately take over as research leaders. In-service training, scholarships, and fellowships are made available to talented local people, many of whom take advanced degrees in the States and then return to become agricultural research and administration leaders in their home countries.

Rockefeller began in Mexico in 1943; its North American personnel, who lived there long enough to learn Spanish well and to adapt to Latin customs, were then used to launch the Colombian and later the Chilean programs. As Mexicans became more and more able to run the program themselves, they replaced North Americans. One such is my good friend, Dr. Antonio Rodríguez, now head of the plant pathology department in Mexico's Office of Special Studies. Dr. Rodríguez received his Ph.D. at Purdue University, studying on a Rockefeller fellowship. Now back in his native Mexico, he has a leading position in that country's continuing campaign for better food supplies and better health. And he has nothing but praise for the Rockefeller Foundation.

The Foundation stresses the need for working *with* and not *for* the people being assisted; personally, I feel that its success,

74

in public relations, at least, lies in working *with* rather than *over* them. I say this because of the local acceptance of yet another group of experts—the professional consultants hired by Latin American governments. In Honduras, for instance, Brown and Root engineers are helping the highway department in a major program of road construction and Harza engineers are supervising the construction of the Río Lindo hydroelectric project. Both the chiefs of the departments involved and the Minister of Public Works laud the consultants as experts and as people. On the other hand, criticism is rampant against numerous technical experts sent here by our government.

I suspect that the difference lies in the fact that to the government experts the Latins they serve are *wards,* whereas the commercial consultants regard them as *accounts.* Furthermore, there is what Latins call "the boomerang effect" in U.S. government aid: the experts of the old ICA (now AID, Administration for International Development) who come here are often exempt from local income taxes and also from customs duties on their personal effects, including highly taxed automobiles. This, of course, is piddling in comparison with grants and loans in the tens of millions, but its psychological effects are great and it is just more grist for the ever active Communist propaganda mill.

It seems to me that technical aid can best be rendered along the lines established by the Rockefeller Foundation. Where individual consultants rather than full-fledged programs are needed, we would do better to grant the funds so that individual governments could select and hire their own man. As *their* man rather than ours, he will be eminently more acceptable.

There may also be areas in which technical aid should be given only in the form of training programs in the States to which Latin specialists can be invited. I think of the current howls in the Honduran press over the presence here of a U.S. police expert (variously identified as "a Foreign Service Reserve Officer" and "an FBI agent") who is teaching modern methods to local security police. "Is this not," critics ask, "sub-

75

mission of the repressive organs of our country to a foreign power? Is not John Donney's 'double role' a dangerous intervention?" (Part of the protest, of course, comes from the Communists, more of whom have been apprehended in recent months, perhaps because of Mr. Donney's help. But another part comes from non-Communist nationalists, who fear our influence in such a sensitive area as public security. A wiser plan would have been to arrange a course in Washington for Honduran security police officials, thus avoiding the stigma of "intervention" for this aid effort.)

Even if we avoid the antipathies that have been and are being aroused by much of our technical aid, we still face those caused by our nonprofessional representatives here: the salesmen, small businessman, missionaries and, as ever, tourists. In my experience, these diplomats without portfolio have on a few occasions done much good for the U.S. image in Latin America. But more often, much more often, they have done great harm.

September 15, Independence Day in Honduras.

All around me, the sounds of celebration: firecrackers popping, bands playing, horns beeping, people laughing and shouting. On this day 139 years ago, Honduras fought free of Spanish rule. Since then, it has moved from the grip of one dictator to that of another, meanwhile serving as the scene of 135 revolutions—almost one a year. Now, under a freely elected, truly democratic regime, the people really celebrate this day.

A parade clangs by, flowered floats, bestreamered trucks and cars, roaring motorcycles topped by fluttering flags, dissonant but enthusiastic high school bands.

In front of me, a pair of North American tourists. Each holds a 35mm camera; each carries, slung from his shoulder, a loaded gadget bag. But neither shoots a picture.

"Pretty crummy," one says.

"Yeah," replies the other. "Mexico puts on a helluva lot better show."

76

Several bystanders who understand English turn to look at them; then, with the ineffable raised-eyebrow Latin shrug, go back to watching the parade. The tourists elbow their way through the crowd, looks of petulant annoyance on their faces. Soon after, the parade is past, the crowd breaks up, and I leave too.

The festive feeling pervades the city, but inside the hotel bar the one table of customers is sullen. They are traveling salesmen from the States with nothing to do until the fiesta ends and the stores reopen. They are a little tight, and a little loud.

I sit at the bar and sip a cool *Salva Vida* beer. After the heat of the street it's a real lifesaver.

The bartender turns on the radio, fiddles with dials, tunes in a patriotic speech, loud. The voice sounds like Foreign Minister Alvarado Puerto. He talks of the glories of independence, reminding his audience that every nation in the Americas, from the United States to Argentina, fought for and won its independence; that all owe much to the United States, which set the early example.

"Shut that junk off!" one of the salesmen shouts. Then, to his companions, he mutters, "Damn people talk all the time. . . ."

The bartender turns down the radio, his hand trembling but his face, trained to its task, composed.

My wife rides in a fruit company car with a group of other North American women on their way to San Pedro to shop. They pass through Old Lima, the town where the chauffeur's family lives.

"What a filthy town!" one of the women exclaims. "I'm afraid every time I ride through it."

"I can't understand how anyone can live here," another says.

"They don't know the difference," explains the third. "They're more like animals than people."

The car lurches slightly as the chauffeur, white-knuckled,

grips the wheel hard. My wife, sitting next to him, knowing that he understands English, embarrassed for him, whispers an apology. He smiles.

"I understand, Doña Gina."

He understands, but she does not. Why, she asks me that night, why must we be like that?

I ride with a visiting compatriot back to the coast. He, heading for a business appointment, wears white shirt and slacks; I, along for the ride, in my usual khakis and tired old felt hat. We stop in the halfway town, Siguatepeque.

"Want you to meet some friends," he says. "Good people. They're with the Mission here."

We turn off the highway and down a bumpy street. Ahead of us is the unbelievably blue sky of the tropics at high altitudes and the peculiar crumpled mountains, like green blotters tossed aside unused, that are uniquely Honduran. And then we come to the house, a bit of Rochelle Park, N.J., picture window fronting on the street, boxer chained in the yard, cyclone fence all around.

He parks the Jeep in the driveway and leaves me there while he looks for his friends. I rest in the seat, hat tipped over my eyes, enjoying the cool, storing it up against the coastal heat soon to come. A station wagon approaches, shiny, new. Inside, two children, a boy and a girl, and their mother, driving. All blond, all shiny, new.

The boy looks at the Jeep blocking the driveway, at me, within, doing nothing. "Tell the *muchacho* to move the car," he says. His mother honks the horn, first a tentative toot, then a blast.

"*Muchacho!*" she calls, her accent poor but her tone of command unmistakable. "Move the car."

In the clear air I see the impatience in her eyes, the frown lines, chronic, between her brows.

I move the car, fuming, fumbling with the gearshift, inept.

And I know, a little, of how my friends here feel about my countrymen, and why.

78

7

The Image of the United States

In addition to the unpleasant picture of the United States
and her people created by our representatives in Latin America,
we must somehow live down the larger and equally ugly history
of Saxons in general (or what we call "Westerners") and the
projection of our internal culture as seen by Latins, especially
the intellectual leaders.

As Toynbee has noted, Russia was invaded by Western armies
in 1610, 1709, 1812, 1915, and 1941; Africa saw its people
kidnaped and sold into Western slavery; South Africa suffered
a British aggressive war in 1899–1902, and Spain an American
aggressive war, disguised as sympathy for Cubans, in 1898.
Germans are Saxons, too—and they attacked their neighbors
in World Wars I and II. The Americans Indians were killed or
swept aside to make room for Saxons and their Negro slaves;
Asians have suffered the incursions of Western missionaries,
merchants, and military since the 15th century. And meanwhile,
Westerners have occupied and exploited "the lion's share of the
world's last vacant lands in the Americas, Australia, New
Zealand and South and East Africa."[1]

Ancient history? Perhaps. And offset, since 1945 at least, by
such events as the Dutch evacuation of Indonesia, the British
evacuation of India, Pakistan, Burma, and Ceylon, and the
world-wide aid efforts of the United States. But for over four
centuries the West has been the aggressor in the world, and few
peoples have avoided suffering at Western hands. Four centuries

[1] Arnold Toynbee, "Russia and the West," *Harper's,* March 1953.

of aggression are not forgotten in less than two decades of non-aggression, especially when the latter often seems like more of the same, disguised as "trade."

Looking at the United States from outside, Latins do not see too reassuring a picture even in our period of greatest altruism.

They see the nation that perfected and dropped the A-bomb and hear the man who made the final decision, former President Truman, declare, "I had no qualms about using it," adding that the United States would use the H-bomb in the same way should the world get into turmoil again.[2]

They see the nation that allowed a Senator McCarthy to abrogate civil liberties and create countrywide hysteria for three years, during which time most U.S. politicians, including then-President Eisenhower, most U.S. newspapers, and most U.S. citizens found the assent of silence the safest policy.

They see the nation that is trying to sell them democracy implement its Negroes' quest for equality, in James Wechsler's words, "with all deliberate lack of speed."[3]

They see the nation that professes hatred for all forms of totalitarianism play "footsie" with a dozen Latin American dictators and then, repenting in its own hemisphere, back undemocratic regimes in South Korea, Taiwan, South Vietnam, and Pakistan, to say nothing of Franco's Spain.

They see the nation that is giving them help against poverty and unemployment explain away the misery of millions of its own with the magic phrase "business cycles," and fail to cut unemployment, even in good times, below 6–7,000,000.[4]

They see the nation born in dissidence and individualism reach conformity so pervasive that only 26 per cent of its teenagers often disagree with their peers, and half of whom believe

[2] TV interview with Edward R. Murrow, February 1958, cited by James A. Wechsler in *Reflections of an Angry Middle-Aged Editor*, Random House, 1960.

[3] Op. cit.

[4] John Kenneth Galbraith, *The Affluent Society*, Houghton-Mifflin Company, 1958.

80

large masses of people are not capable of determining what is good for them.[5]

They see the nation whose "free enterprise" is limited by admitted collusion among some of the largest corporations and whose union labor is exploited by greedy leaders, many of whom command as much strength—and amass as much wealth—as almost any of the old-style Latin *caudillos*.

They do not see the guilt-haggled soul searching of many politicians, scientists, and ordinary citizens over the bomb; they do not see the day-to-day democracy of numerous national and local leaders; they do not see the heart-warming examples, in the North, for the most part, of acceptance of at least some Negroes as first-class citizens; they do not see the elaborate web of international politics that often forces the United States to deal with dictators or lose a whole area to the Communists; they do not see the truly enlightened capitalism of quite a few U.S. corporations and the selfless dedication of numerous labor leaders.

Why not?

Because it is press tradition to report the aberrant rather than the routine; because Communist propaganda exults in our failures and says nothing, naturally, of our successes; because anti-Yanqui feeling serves as a filter on Latin Americans' perceptions, screening out the good and allowing the bad to come through. I doubt that the most intensive efforts of such agencies as the U.S. Information Agency could begin to offset this negative image, but I am sure that until we recognize the existence of the problem we will have not the slightest chance of solving it.

Similarly, most North Americans who come here do not see the romanticism of many Latins; their constant philosophical approach to life, no matter how rich or poor their circumstances; their freedom from convention despite *costumbre* and Catholicism; their deep interest in people; their infinite loyalty

[5] H. H. Remmers and D. H. Radler, *The American Teenager*, Bobbs-Merrill Company, 1957.

81

as friends. Instead, they see what looks like laziness (mañana); they see trash thrown out the door and cigarettes squelched on the floor; they see "moral looseness" ("With a Latin girl," a visiting North American once assured me, "it's not whether, but when"); they see the negative passion of blood feuds without knowing the positive passion of loyalty that triggered them.

Of course Latins aren't perfect—they're people. I live with them and daily see things I would prefer to have changed. For my tastes, Latin Americans play their radios too loud; they are overly passionate politically; they impose too many visitors (from babes in arms to patriarchs) on the sick and grief-stricken. Because of overstress on the value of the male (*el culto del machismo*), Latin boys tend to be little monsters, undisciplined and disrespectful. (Only in rare cases, however, does their proud young maleness organize itself into teen-age gangs à la New York and Chicago; but Latins are, fortunately, much less organized than we in every sphere.) Although they make attentive, affectionate fathers, many Latin men are inconsiderate of and often openly disrespectful toward their wives, treating them more like servants than like life companions.

I would prefer to see these things different than they are, yet I do not set about changing them: as their guest, I have no missionary right. (Neither do our missionaries, in my opinion.) When a man says "My house is yours," he does not mean for you to start rearranging the furniture. And that, of course, is what we always try to do.

In reaction to this patronizing impoliteness, and to the negative image they hold of our nation as a nation, many more Latins than we officially recognize gravitate toward Communism as "the other answer." There are not excessive numbers of card-carrying Communists here, nor are there very many Russophiles as such. But there are Communist sympathizers galore, as the demonstrations throughout Latin America during the Punta del Este meeting in January of 1962 amply demonstrated.

Why?

Partly because of the unfortunate human tendency to think in "either-or" terms: if not with the United States, then with the Russians. (And we accent this tendency when our various pundits declare, as so many seem to be declaring lately, that there are no neutrals—a country is either "with us or agin us." See John Fischer's "A Hopeful Letter to Fowler Hamilton" in the November 1961 *Harper's,* or Max Ascoli's editorial and George Bailey's article, "They Call Themselves Neutrals" in *The Reporter* for September 28, 1961.) The other motivating force is the Russian promise to the hungry nations: that communism will give them the strength to stand up against the United States, the same strength it gave Russia, the same strength that has put the Cold War initiative in Russian hands for more than a decade.

Unpleasant as it may be, we would do well to recognize that this is the dynamic that turned Cuba's revolution into a victory for the Communists—the appeal of standing up against the United States. That same appeal is what made ardent Communists out of numerous Latin intellectuals.

Take César Vallejo of Peru, recognized during his lifetime as one of the finest poets writing in Spanish, seen now, a quarter century after his death, as one of the two or three greatest writers Latin America has ever produced.

As a young man Vallejo was strongly aroused by dictatorial oppression in his own country and by the desperate plight of the vast Indian population. Conscious of his own partial kinship with the Indians, he espoused their cause and, while still in his twenties, was jailed for being an "incendiary." In 1928, at the age of 35, he left Peru, disillusioned, never to return.

He went to Paris, and then to Russia, finding the latter country a nation rebuilding itself after a long and bloody revolution, a nation dedicated to the cause of the poor, a nation of hope.

He told his wife of this "decisive fact in his life and work: the ills of mankind have a remedy."

Then came the Spanish Civil War. Aware now of his Spanish as well as his Indian heritage, having resided in Spain for some time, and having published there with success, Vallejo fought for the Loyalist cause against the Fascist insurgents led by Franco. He saw Franco receive aid from Germany and Italy;

83

he saw France and England remain neutral; he saw what little help the Loyalists got coming from Russia and the International Brigade, an idealist band composed of liberals from all over the world, many of them Communists, many others later to become Communists. He saw the war go on, and saw it lost, and saw Franco's government recognized by the West, but not by Russia, and later actively aided by the United States.

His Communist leanings were confirmed.

Note that Vallejo's novel about Yanqui exploitation of Peruvian miners (*Tungsteno,* 1931) was written before he became a Communist, although it was not published until afterward; and that it was subsequent to this work that he published *Rusia,* a eulogy of the Red revolution—Vallejo was anti-Yanqui first, Communist later.

Still a confirmed Communist, Vallejo died in Europe in 1938. He did not see the blood purges in Russia, the takeover of Poland, Czechoslovakia, and Hungary, the beginning of the Cold War. His continuing communism, to me, is understandable.

But not that of the people today who laud Vallejo's politics as well as his poetry, including the director of Lima's Gallery of Contemporary Art; the winner of Peru's national poetry award and editor of "Tasks of Peruvian Thought"; and the wife of the editor of "Peruvian Letters," herself a doctor of letters.

Recently I asked a Costa Rican friend of a mine, a teacher and a poet in his own right, how he would account for the communism of such people—and his own belief in communism.

"We tend to be rebels," he said, smiling. "Maybe it is in our blood, or maybe it is because government, in most of our history, meant exploitation and suppression. The church helped that suppression, so we tend to be anti-clerical. Your government and your big business helped, too, so we are also anti-Yanqui.

"But most of all, I think, it is because our intellectuals feel that emotion is basic to thought, while yours act as if they believe one cannot think until all emotion is dead. Vallejo talks of individual men and women and thereby becomes universal— your intellectuals talk of 'humanity,' of 'progress'—and these

84

are abstractions, far distant from the *pueblo*—and thereby become particular." (In my mind I recalled the comparison made once by André Maurois between Brazil's foremost writer, Machado de Assis, whose biographer said he "hated mankind and loved the individual" and Woodrow Wilson, about whom Maurois wrote, "He loved mankind and hated men."[6])

"But what about Poland, Czechoslovakia, Hungary?" I asked. *"This* is 'liking people'? And what about Cuba—do you really think the *guajiro* is any better off now than he was under Batista?"

My friend smiled. "Propaganda," he said. "None of these things are as bad as your press reports them. But the exploitation of your banana companies, this I have seen in my own country. And the Marines in Nicaragua, I have seen them, too. Pablo Neruda [another fine poet and a Communist leader in his native Chile] writes of that: 'There, there are bananas to defend and not liberties; for this, Somoza will do.' Your press wants us to believe that your aims are pure and democratic; why would it not try to make us believe that the Russians are worse than they are?"

Although I know many instances of prejudice and superficiality on the part of our press, I know none of downright propaganda, and doubt that any U.S. wire service release or major newspaper report is written with influencing people in mind— quite the opposite, in fact. On the other hand, the highly visible errors we have committed in Latin America remain largely unreported in our press; that silence in itself seems suspicious to Latins. And finally, whatever errors the Russians commit are distant (except in the case of Cuba)—by the time a country learns for itself what communism is all about, it is already too late.

No amount of money budgeted for the USIA can offset this imbalance. Latin America will never be solidly in our camp until we right our own errors, repair the damage we have already done, and move in a direction that is acceptable to Latins as

[6] André Maurois, *My Latin-American Diary,* Falcon Press, London, 1953.

well as advantageous to us. It may already be too late—or there may be inherent conflicts between the Latin and the Saxon personalities that override any amount of good will on our part. (Note that José Hernández had certainly not seen too many gringos in his native Argentina when he wrote "How big and ugly is the gringo!" back in 1872. And Spanish author Ramón del Valle Inclán was reacting to appearances, not events, when he described Saxons, in his *Sonata de Estío,* "The Saxon race is the most worthless on earth. Contemplating their grotesque and weak fights . . . I felt a new face of shame: zoological shame.")

In general, Latins are more southerly peoples than Saxons: most of them live in tropical areas, while most of us live in temperate or frigid lands. It is a truism, which is supported by anyone who has traveled, that people of warm countries tend to be more leisurely, perhaps because they need not work so hard to secure food, clothing, and shelter. (In addition, the vast bulk of the population in Latin America is suffering from malnutrition, worms, amebas, and other dietary diseases which sap energy and ambition.) Here one finds the slower time sense (we say "last-minute bulletin"; they, "last hour news") and the greater accent on the social amenities—except promptness. This is the basis of the mañana attitude we deplore as shiftlessness and utilize as the central theme in our perception of "the Latin American ethos." In return, Latins tend to see our efficiency, our preoccupation with "the job," as cold and dehumanized, more machine than man.

Another source of Latin politeness, which we view as overeffusiveness, is the fact that most of them come from relatively crowded areas; in cramped quarters, courtesy is a necessity if murder is to be avoided. Note, for example, that Japan, one of the world's most overpopulated lands, has evolved a veritable cult of courtesy extending even to such a moment of lonely despair as that of hara-kiri. Northerners in general have more land per person, more air; partially as a result of this, their attitude is more breezy. And it looks, to Latins, like insulting familiarity. Daily, I find myself charmed at hearing Latins who have known

86

each other all their lives refer to one another as "don Luís" and "doña Tina"; to hear customers entering a store ask permission of the owner to do so; to hear a mayor or a large landowner walk away from a *campesino* with a "By your leave." And daily, Latins are offended to meet gringos who don't offer to shake hands, who slip into first names on first acquaintance, and who end a conversation simply by walking away or with a flip "See ya."

In general it is true that natural obstacles to industrialization, which we view as the only real progress, are greater in tropical lands than they are to the north. In Latin America huge mountain ranges impede the development of transportation and communications systems; lack of cheap fuel deposits and of cheap metal lodes militates against the initiation of the basic heavy industry, steel; where they exist, the distance of such deposits from natural sites of manufacture works against the utilization of steel even were it produced in quantity. Furthermore, we should remember Latin America did not achieve independence until a half century later than we, and this battle was followed by a full century of internal strife and despotism that forestalled any hope for industrial development. As a result of these factors, Latin America lags far behind us in the development of systems capable of competing in an industrial world—the very systems we prize and respect most, perhaps because they are largely ours.

Reacting, we tend to blame them for their "failure," to view them as inferior because their achievement doesn't match ours. Hardly an attitude guaranteed to achieve popularity, here or anywhere else in the world!

There is also the "color angle." In our culture, white is the color of purity; this may be reflection or cause of our belief in the superiority of the fair-skinned person, manifested in such phrases as "the white man's burden," and in our continuing inhumanity toward our own Negroes. Most Latins are darker than we; therefore we tend to see them as inferior on the basis of race and color (and some of us have gone so far as to say, with novelist Kenneth Roberts, that Latins in general—he spoke of

Central Americans—are "worthless, futile, good-for-nothing mongrels"). Caste and color are related in Latin America, with the outstanding exception of Brazil: the leaders are the *trigueños,* the followers the *indios* and *morenos.* But to us even a *trigueño* is darker than—and therefore lesser than—a "white man," although he may well be a far better man.

In recent years our accent Stateside on production and consumption, on group rather than individual thought and action, and on the cult of personality has contributed to an ugly atmosphere of anti-intellectualism. In large part, Adlai Stevenson could not be elected President because he is, clearly, an intellectual (he is also the best-liked gringo in Latin America, although he has never had a chance to make material contribution to any economy here); President Kennedy achieved election by hiding the fact that he, too, is an intellectual. But the Governor of Puerto Rico and the President of Colombia are intellectuals, both liberal essayists and journalists; the President of Honduras was his country's foremost pediatrician and a medical sociologist; the former President of Costa Rica, José Figueres, is an economist and MIT-trained engineer. Other current and past leaders are of similar stature. In Latin America, "a man may be writing poetry on Friday and become President or Minister of Foreign Affairs the following Sunday."[7]

This political acceptability of the cultured man in Latin America rests on a solid foundation of culture among the people. Noting the illiteracy statistics, we tend to write the area off as barbaric—even Bertrand Russell once called it that—but the fact is that those who can read, do, and derive considerably more from their reading than we seem to from ours.

I sat entranced one afternoon in a little Mexican *cantina* listening to the bartender and a customer, a truck driver, discuss the philosophy of Kierkegaard and its relation to anti-clericalism in their country. During their conversation I heard references to Heidegger, Sartre, and Maritain, among others, and found myself acquiring an education in existentialism that had theretofore been sadly lacking.

[7] Salvador de Madariaga, op. cit.

88

Nor is my experience, of which this is just one anecdote, in any way unique. André Maurois, for instance, traveling in South America in 1953, described his Argentine chauffeur: "An astonishing person . . . speaks French well; in addition to being a chauffeur, he is a journalist and writer, and knows everything from the cure for angina to the latest book that must be read. . . ."[8]

Our ignorance of the cultural richness of Latin America forms part of the patronizing image we project here. Seeking data for this chapter in reference works written in English, I had virtually no luck; few of the leading intellectual lights of the area could be found even in such a thick volume as the Columbia Encyclopedia (1950 edition), which mentioned the town of Vallejo, California, but not the Number One or Number Two poet of this half of the hemisphere! Such a formidable work as Crane Brinton's *Ideas and Men,* a survey of the development of Western thought, fails even to list Latin America in the index—apparently Western thought excludes everything south of the border. Another huge tome, *Great Stories of All Nations,* by Lieber and Williams, devotes only 28 of its over 1,000 pages to Latin American tales, choosing only 5, none of those by the most distinguished *cuentistas.*

Perhaps this ignorance stems in part from the language barrier and from the fact that our historical as well as our linguistic tradition is English. Spanish is universally considered the easiest to learn of all the Romance languages, if not of all civilized tongues. Yet even those of our people who come to live and work here rarely learn to speak Spanish well; perhaps they feel it isn't worth it. But to be forever unaware of the complex simplicity of a Vallejo is, in itself, a high price to pay for continued ignorance. . . .

Considering all of these factors, it is apparent that the problem of human relations between Latins and gringos reflects some of the inherent frictions between "white men" and "men of color"; some of those between "haves" and "have-nots"; and some of those between men whose logic dominates their emo-

[8] André Maurois, op. cit.

tions and men whose emotions are an indispensable part of their logic. We cannot change our color, or theirs, except through a long process of genetic mingling; we cannot change our relative richness and their relative poverty except by a lengthy process of social and economic development. Neither of these processes really has a chance of beginning until we mix our technical superiority with an emotional range and true tolerance that far transcends the hypocrisy of the Dale Carnegie system.

We have a hint of how it can be done from the gringos who are accepted here as *"muy buena gente."* There are some in every Latin American country; their fame, in some cases, passes national borders.

Examining the behavior of several of these real "good will ambassadors," one sees certain similarities. They are, almost uniformly, permanent residents, as much interested in this part of the world as in their home country. They are, almost uniformly, intellectuals—archeologists, agricultural scientists, educators. They all speak the language, poorly in some cases, well in others. But they speak it, and do not demand that Latins speak English. They all adapt to local food, drink, and housing gracefully and comfortably—not as an act, not "going native," but as a normal reaction of appreciation or even preference. They are all courteous people; as with Latins, this courtesy may be only verbal, and may cover urges far from polite, but it is used constantly as a means of greasing the gears of human relations.

More important than these readily visible characteristics, however, are two more subtle and much more significant personality factors. The first of these is that these "good gringos" are not organization men—they are individuals. They do not derive their identity through the simple and artificial means of belonging to something, but through the more difficult and meaningful method of working out for themselves who they are and what their role is in the world at large. They are not joiners, but seekers. Because of this they are not provincial, not nationalistic, not racist; they are able to relate to other

90

people simply as people rather than as foreigners and strangers.

Taking personal responsibility for the basic problem of their own existence, these people are able to feel and express a personal need for what Latins as people can give them. Thus their relations are a mutual interchange, not a constant, lofty giving or a constant greedy taking. And mutual interchange is the very basis of that otherwise indescribable phenomenon called love. They love, these men and women, and they are loved in return.

Most diplomats, businessmen, salesmen, and journalists are, by nature, organization men; few can be expected to feel other than as joiners—they are people who have passed the responsibility for their own identity on to the group. Thus few of these official representatives can be expected to have the fundamental personality structure that is basic to being *"muy buena gente"* in Latin eyes. But the selection of people to serve here in any capacity should be made on the basis of approaching as closely as possible this basic trait and the other, simpler characteristics mentioned earlier. The training given such people should stress, more than any other factor, the human side of their daily lives in Latin America.

A hard job? Yes. But no harder than finding $20 billion to aid Latin America's social and economic development, and potentially more rewarding for all concerned. If we fail in this job, the $20 billion will be wasted and the Communists will take over here, as we shall see in intimate detail in the next chapter.

8

The Communists Move In

Jean-Paul Sartre, existentialist philosopher and writer of consummate power albeit of Communist prejudice, was talking (in *Sartre on Cuba,* Ballantine, 1961) of returning by plane to Havana from a trip to the interior. He saw the sight that many of us have seen—Havana at night. He expressed it this way:

"Already we were coming down into a cluster of jewels— diamonds, rubies, turquoises. The memory of a recent conversation returned to me at that moment, preventing me from admiring that archipelago of fire against the black glass of the sea. These riches were not Cuban."

M. Sartre goes on to explain that a North American company supplied Cuba with electricity, as it still does much of Latin America, repatriating its profits. "The fires grew larger," he continues, "the precious stones swelled, became sparkling fruits; the cloth of night was torn away. Almost touching the ground, I saw the lights appear, but I said to myself, 'It's foreign gold that's shining.'

"I had misunderstood everything. What I took to be signs of wealth were, in fact, signs of dependence and poverty. At each ringing of the telephone, at each twinkling of neon, a small piece of a dollar left the island and formed, on the American continent, a whole dollar with the other pieces that were waiting for it."

Whether one likes the direction the Cuban Revolution has taken or not—and I do not—here is a succinct description of what led up to it. Communists moved in to enslave Cubans because of an environment propitious for revolution and for communism: an environment we had created, as I pointed out in Chapter 2. Cuba would not be a Red satellite today, a threat to our prestige, peace of mind, and physical security, were it not for our own serious errors there in the distant and recent past. We sowed the seed; the Commies reaped the harvest.

Today, although our State Department admits to having made "certain errors in Cuba," we still do not understand the factors that led to the creation of a Communist state in our own hemisphere. And we still refuse to understand how that single seed center is utilizing our continuing "certain errors" to spread the Red blot wider and wider here. Working now through Havana, the Communists are infiltrating all of Latin America. Using our continuing financial exploitation and our usual arrogance to their political advantage, they are convincing more and more of our Latin American neighbors that their future resides, not with us, but with the Russians. If we cannot understand this and counter it, all Latin America will ultimately fall to the Communists. And if it falls, we fall, too.

In Chapter 2 I described how our behavior in Cuba established an environment within which the Communists could work to take over the island. Then they were working at a distance, with the difficulties that distance always imposes. Now they have Cuba and own, right here, a center of infection from which the germ of communism can spread and reproduce itself in the already anti-gringo agar that is Latin America. In this chapter, let us examine exactly how they are taking advantage of their new opportunity.

Four Central American Presidents interviewed last January by *U.S. News & World Report* had this to say about the problem:

Panama's Roberto F. Chiari—"We are confronting an extraordinary force of agitators who are exerting all their efforts to confuse the democratic powers. Numerically, the Communists in Panama are not many, but in quality and organization they are strong. . . ."

Nicaragua's Luís A. Somoza—"We now have a little monster in Central America. . . . We have captured arms that were sent from Cuba."

Guatemala's Miguel Ydígoras Fuentes—"Time is running out for our side. . . ."

Honduras' Ramón Villeda Morales—"I confess that we are incapable of overcoming the Castro infiltration into Honduras by ourselves. The democratic countries should abandon their passive attitude."

Let us examine Communist activity, first in Honduras (whose Director General of Public Security calls his country "the focal point for the development of Communist plans in Central America") and then in Guatemala, the area's most populous republic and one that has recently had (1954) a Communist government.

Honduras' President, Dr. Ramón Villeda Morales, was educated as a physician but has always been inclined toward the social aspects of medicine. Since his election in 1957 he has concentrated on health, education, and welfare for his country's nearly 2 million people. Every month, a new public work has been dedicated. During his 3½ years in office, Villeda has built more schools, health centers, roads, and bridges than Honduras previously had in its entire history. He has given workers a labor code that assures their right to collective bargaining, guarantees a minimum wage, hospital benefits, vacation with pay, and terminal leave, and provides for full court hearings in case of unresolved disputes.

He has also negotiated development loans totaling more millions than had previously been available to the country throughout its history. These loans are being used for such purposes as the construction of a hydroelectric plant on Río Blanco, which will ultimately supply more electricity than is now available in Honduras, Guatemala, and El Salvador combined; and to link formerly isolated cities by all-weather roads.

Before Fidel's *barbudos* swept into power in Cuba, Villeda faced sporadic armed attacks by right-wing elements eager to re-establish dictatorship. He handled these readily with support from the army, university students, workers, and the general public. (Some of the latter, hastily armed in July 1959 when a revolt broke out in Tegucigalpa, have recently been discovered to be Communists and to still possess the weapons issued so hurriedly in defense of the country.)

Since the Cuban Revolution, however, Villeda's government has been the target of a campaign of left-wing agitation that has swung the students against him, made army support questionable, aroused workers to the brink of illegal strike, and caused the general public to doubt his ability. Meanwhile, his country has served as the entry point for Red arms, money, agents, and propaganda sent from Havana, and still serves as the hub of the network of Communist agitation in the Caribbean area.

Although the Communist Party as such is illegal here, it operates fairly openly and its members are, for the most part, known. In addition, there are innumerable pro-Communist groups that contribute to the Red campaign here, ranging from newspapers and radio stations to unions of schoolteachers and student organizations. Cleanup attempts go on, but because of the popularity of Fidel Castro and the unpopularity of the United States, they lack public support. Thus do the Communists turn the national pride and naïveté of a whole republic against itself. So far the formula has worked so well that the nation's leading paper, *El Día,* has sadly commented in several editorials, "There seems to be no way of fighting the Communists."

The political calendar of Honduras over the past two years is an almanac of intrigue. Examining it, one can see that the Reds are operating here. More important, one can learn just *how* they operate.

February 1960—Left-wing Congressman Ildefonso Orellana Bueso of San Pedro Sula, economic capital of the nation, tells the Congress that armed attack on Cuba is being prepared here under the auspices of Home Minister Jorge Bueso Arias and the United Fruit Company, largest company in the country and the major factor in the national economy.

Without presenting documentation, Orellana declares that

95

UFCo's five airfields on the north coast are to be the springboard of a move to overthrow Castro and restore Dictator Fulgencio Batista to power in Cuba. He avers that arms are being flown in from Guatemala by a pilot from San Pedro named Elias Hasbun, who is "in the pay of Home Minister Bueso."

Despite the lack of documentation and the patent absurdity of the charges, an investigating committee is appointed by President Villeda. On it are the ministers of justice, labor, and public works; the attorney general; the director of civil aviation; three congressmen, including Orellana; and the president of the Red-lining Federation of University Students, Carlos Falk.

After on-the-spot probing, the committee reports that all of Orellana's charges are false: the UFCo. airfields, all duly registered, are used for agricultural spray planes; the "tanks of explosives" are drums of a plant fungicide; and "Pilot Hasbun" is no pilot, for he has never flown a plane.

The report is signed by every member of the committee except Congressman Orellana. Congress votes to adopt the report and the case is officially closed.

Thereafter, among the capital papers only *El Cronista,* vigorous supporter of Castro and constant critic of the Villeda regime and the United States, continues to circulate the charges. So does Student Leader Falk who now declares himself "unconvinced" that Orellana's charges were unfounded.

In San Pedro thousands turn out for a pro-Castro demonstration at which Congressman Orellana and his unfounded charges are firmly supported and the Villeda government and the United States are roundly denounced. The demonstration was arranged and led by known Communists.

Meanwhile, the directors of two student newspapers known for their extreme left-wing stance fly to Mexico to attend a meeting of their colleagues from all over Latin America; here they introduce and see passed a resolution condemning AP and UPI, U.S. wire services, and lauding *Prensa Latina,* Castro's mouthpiece.

April 1960—At the personal invitation of Fidel Castro, the director of *El Cronista* flies to Havana. Twelve days later he

96

is followed by ten other Hondurans, including Congressman Orellana and leaders of the Federation of University Students. This group was invited, all expenses paid, by Raúl Castro, Fidel's brother.

Meanwhile, Honduras receives a special "trade mission" from Egypt. Its first act: to decorate President Villeda with the Grand Cordon of the Order of Egypt. Its second act: a talk at the National University by Dr. Ibrahin Hagras, lauding the Russians for their favorable loan to Nasser for the Aswan Dam ("This is not Russian economic or political intervention") and eulogizing Egyptian land reform ("The country people are tranquil now").

Editorializes *El Cronista,* "Only the message of the Cuban people has been received so warmly by cultural circles here. . . . The enthusiasm with which our people have received the Cuban and Egyptian rebellions indicates the majority desire for the same end."

Home from Havana, *El Cronista* Director Alejandro Valladares begins a series of editorials praising the Cuban Revolution and defending it against the charge of "Communism." "Ninety-eight percent of the people are for it," Valladares declares.

May 1960—The First Congress of University Students of Central America and Panama meets here. The Congress devotes four days to condemning "economic imperialism," censuring AP, UPI, and the leading dailies of the area for "untruthfulness," and shouting support for Fidel Castro and his *Prensa Latina.*

Chief official act: voting to tie in with Prague's International Student Union—a pure Communist organization. Why? Perhaps because most of the young rebels in the group have already visited Havana, where they were wined, dined, and made much of—and where they were assured that *they* would be their countries' leaders when "the day" arrives. Heady wine indeed for a youngster to whom nobody else pays much attention. . . .

Meanwhile, the propaganda campaign grows more heated—

97

and its Communist sponsorship becomes more apparent. Celebrating its sixth anniversary, the illegal but ever active Communist Party of Honduras boldly letters on walls all over the capital city: *"Hondureño.* Fight Yankee imperialism, your principal enemy. *Partido Comunista de Honduras. 6 Aniv."*

Echoing this cry, *El Cronista* editorializes on May 21: "There is not—there cannot be—danger in the Cuban Revolution. The danger is in the entrails of the powerful economic interests that have acted like stupid Phoenicians in the Spanish-speaking part of America that still prays to Jesus Christ.[1] . . . We will learn English, but patriotically, we will speak it poorly!"

Then Cuban Ambassador Silvio Sorhegui, who had long offended the Honduran Government by meddling in internal affairs and by making invidious comparisons between this country and the new Cuba, was quietly asked to leave. He does—but he returns "to pick up some personal effects," taking advantage of this final visit by delivering a "literary lecture" at the National University exalting Cuban Communist Poet Rubén Martínez Villena and his work.

The source of the agitation which is unsettling Honduras is obvious from the context. In case there should be any doubt, however, departing Ambassador Sorhegui somehow manages to leave behind his expense account for the month of May. It lists $9500 for "students and labor," $2500 for "press," and $2500 for "politics."

That the "press" portion goes to *El Cronista* is also obvious —but then Director of Security Carlos Rívas Córdoba makes it official when he declares publicly that *Cronista* "receives money and instructions from Moscow." To date, the charge remains uncontested.

June 1960—The Nationalist Party, Villeda's right-wing opposition, begins to raise a cry demanding that Honduras sever relations with Cuba. Various members of Villeda's own Liberal Party second this, accusing their chief of "swimming in two waters"—democracy and pro-U.S. sentiment and Castroism

---

[1] Almost a direct quote from Rubén Darío's poem "dedicated" to Theodore Roosevelt as the instigator of the revolt in Panama.

with its Communist leaning. Apparently ignoring the furor, Villeda takes no action. Is the avowedly great friend of the United States and former Ambassador to Washington hypocrite, coward, or good politician? Analysts here and abroad ponder the question.

The campaign goes on . . .

On June 11, 1960, Students Day, the youth of the country celebrate by condemning Villeda, the armed forces, the clergy, the United States. The demonstrations go beyond shouting and sign-waving—in the capital, windows of stores owned by "capitalists" are shattered, and in tiny, usually quiet Ocotopeque, the home of President Villeda's brother is stoned by students shrieking insults against Villeda, his wife, and their families. Student annuals published in Tegucigalpa and San Pedro echo the theme, splattering their pages with vulgar, near-pornographic cartoons.

On June 26, Congressman Orellana, the man who said the Home Minister and United Fruit were preparing to attack Cuba, runs for chief of the incumbent Liberal Party—Villeda's party —in San Pedro, the nation's Number Two city. He is elected by a two to one majority. (In late July the effect of this popularity is more or less nullified when the ten leaders of the Liberal Party of the Cortés District, which includes San Pedro, select Dr. Mario C. Rivas as their chief. Can it be that popular feeling and fear of mob action are preventing Villeda from moving to end the flow of subversion from Cuba? It begins to look that way.)

September 1960—*El Pueblo,* official voice of the Liberal Party, warns that Communists are infiltrating party ranks. (Note that "infiltration" does not mean that Communists are now joining the Liberal Party and somehow assuming control; instead, it indicates that long-time Reds are now allowing their true feelings to show, and are dragging with them the *"tontos útiles,"* or useful fools, who seem always to be available. Apparently, Communists long ago entered political life here—and, one imagines, elsewhere—hiding their actual loyalty until the political climate seemed adapted to their aims. Meanwhile, they assumed positions of major or minor importance, acquired personal fol-

99

lowings, and learned how best to manipulate the publics with which they must deal. One effective technique here: calling themselves Independent Liberals, they label all other members of the incumbent party as Officialists, a term of opprobrium in Latin America, as we shall see later.)

October 1960—The Democratic Honduran Youth Front is formed. Among its aims: "To implant a regime of revolutionary government which will fight for the total independence of the country." Its directors: those Honduran students who visited Cuba, Russia, and Red China in recent months.

December 1960—In Tegucigalpa, the Honduran Revolutionary Party forms; in San Pedro, the Progressive Party of the Honduran People emerges. The aims of both: economic liberation; nationalization of all public services; revocation of such concessions as those of the U.S. fruit companies; relations with Russia and Red China. Since the Communist Party is illegal here, neither of these two groups calls itself that, but their platforms mark them as pro-Red—and their organizers are the anti-U.S. leaders who have visited Cuba, Russia, and Red China recently. Well aware of the true nature of these new parties, the Honduran Government still takes no action against them. Feeling here is so strong that premature vigor against the Communists could result in such national agitation that the Reds might actually take over.

Criticism of this passivity comes from the opposition party, from within Villeda's Liberal Party, and from outside the country. The government of El Salvador announces the discovery of a plot against it led from Tegucigalpa and calls for action on Villeda's part. And *The Miami Herald* criticizes Villeda for trying to play both ends of the U.S.-Cuba tangle against the middle.

The latter story enrages Villeda, who takes to a nationwide radio hookup to label the *Herald* as a member of the United States "most reactionary press, the press that favored . . . isolationism, called the creator of the Good Neighbor Policy a traitor, and maintained an idyll with Latin America's dictators." Predictably, *El Cronista* calls this speech "the most memorable the President has ever made."

When the United States severed relations with Cuba in the early part of 1961, Hondurans discussed doing the same. This was no sympathy move with the United States, but a reaction of annoyance toward the constant recruiting by Havana of Honduran young people who then returned to act as agitators and Communist organizers.

Here is a sample of the way these agitators operate:

Early in 1961 the citizens of the little village of Monjarás petitioned the Honduran Government to award them individual small lots of land—*lotes de familia*—as it had been doing throughout the country while a land reform bill dragged through the preparatory stages.

Before the government could act, Communist student leaders from the capital—trained in Havana since the Cuban Revolution—swept into Monjarás to offer their services to the land-hungry *campesinos*. They organized committees and drew up petitions. With each move, they assured the peasants that "this is how it is done in Cuba; this is how Fidel does it."

Then, when the coveted *lotes* were awarded, as they would have been without the organizing aid of the Communists, the gratitude of the peasants went, not to the government, but to the bright young men who had "helped" them—and to Fidel.

And the committees remained in existence. What their leaders might do with them now, the *campesinos* knew not and cared less.

Here is the first thing they did:

During the discussion of severing diplomatic relations with Cuba, a large advertisement appears in *El Cronista*. It supports Castro and bitterly attacks the United States. It is signed by each of the citizens of Monjarás. Of course most of these people are illiterate; of course most of them cannot even sign their names. But here *are* their names, pegged to a Communist cause and calculated to arouse sympathy from other *campesinos* throughout the country.

This is a recurring technique of Communist agitation in Latin America. Multiply this pattern by the thousands and you begin to see how the Reds, working through Havana, are using for their own purposes the political innocence, illiteracy, and legitimate land hunger of the Latin American peasantry.

The campaign continues . . .

February 1961—Section 4 of the union of the Standard Fruit Co., another of our banana firms here, declares itself publicly against "the aggression of the U.S. toward Cuba," and offers its support to Fidel Castro in his "fight against Yanqui imperialism."

That same month, *El Cronista* publishes an essay by Oscar Castañeda Batres, a Honduran lawyer who lives in Mexico. The essay calls for a national movement for "the second independence—the economic." Castañeda writes, "In Honduras, almost everything we produce is bought by a single buyer, and everything manufactured we buy is sold us by a single seller. This single buyer buys cheap at prices fixed by him; this single seller sells high, at prices fixed by him. What is this except colonialism? What is this except dependence?" (Castañeda is echoing Ecuadorean intellectual Benjamín Carrión, who said almost the same thing earlier in a seminar of political leaders in Bogotá—and Carrión was, of course, parroting the Commie line.)

In late April 1961, Communist demonstrations in favor of Castro were held in the capital. This time, however, instead of two or three thousand, only some 300 people turn out. Has *fidelismo* lost its popular appeal? Or has the usual Communist efficiency failed, this once, to operate? (Some political observers here note recent factional fighting within Honduras' pro-Castro ranks.)

With fortunate timing, on April 21 several thousand citizens demonstrate *against* Fidel in the first major public manifestation of its kind in Honduras.

And on April 22, "bowing to the will of the people," Villeda's government breaks diplomatic relations with Cuba. Privately, a high official of the Liberal Party tells me that Villeda "has wanted to do this for a long time. But he had to have an excuse. And he had to know that it wouldn't lead to a Cuban-style revolution here. . . ."

102

But this does not end the agitation. Honduran youth, already Communist-indoctrinated in Havana, continue their campaign against Villeda and the United States and for Fidel. In April, the University Reform Front, a left-wing student group, condemns the advice being given the Honduran security police by U.S. crime experts (see Chapter 6), declaring this to be "the submission of the repressive organisms of our country to the interests of North American imperialism." And in July it begins to become apparent that the "technicians" who come here to service Czech automobiles and other merchandise from behind the Iron Curtain are, in reality, spies in training; they devote their off-duty time to meeting the students and workers who have visited Havana, Moscow, and Red China and whose names are linked with pro-Red activities, learning the language and the customs of the country, and promising to "be back soon." (Ironically, much of this merchandise is sold by merchants of Arab and Turkish extraction—uniformly called *"turcos"* here—who are reported to be Target Number Two, after gringos, on the Red list of racial agitation.)

In October 1961, a supposed student (32 years old) is found rifling the files of the Army High Command in Tegucigalpa; under questioning he admits that his orders came from the Communists.

In November 1961, the Honduran Revolutionary Party issues a manifesto supporting Castro and criticizing "the governments who are supporting new aggression" against him—which includes all of Central America, united to censure Cuba in the upcoming meeting at Punta del Este.

That same month, Dr. José Ignacio Rasco, a special delegate of the Cuban Revolutionary Council and leader of Cuba's Christian Democrat Movement, reveals in Tegucigalpa that Castro forces, while relations still existed between Cuba and Honduras, had shipped into the country through their embassy here, some 500 pounds of live phosphorus for incendiary bombs (half of which was then transshipped to El Salvador); bazookas, recoilless rifles, grenades, and Czech machine guns; and olive drab military uniforms. In addition, Dr. Rasco reported, the Cuban

103

Embassy had maintained two training camps for guerrilla warriors at Talanga in the hills outside of Tegucigalpa.

In the same month, Honduran Security Chief Tomás Arita Chávez reaffirms that his country was "the focal point of Communist plans in Central America," much to the embarrassment of the administration.

In December 1961, three Honduran lawyers and one university student leave for Red China and Russia, making the usual grand tour from which so many Latin Americans have returned confirmed Communists. The next month, Marco Virgilio Carías, nephew of ex-President Tiburcio Carías Andino (a long-time right-wing leader) goes to join this group. This is the second Carías to make the trip—some years earlier, General Carías' son, Dr. Gonzalo Carías Castillo, had also visited the Iron Curtain "Welcome Wagons."

In January 1962, political pressure explodes in the country's main port, Puerto Cortés, as local citizens openly accuse newly elected Mayor Roberto Valenzuela of being a Communist. On September 15, Honduras' Independence Day, Valenzuela had given a public speech in which he lauded Castro and the Cuban Revolution and criticized the "imperialistic attack" of the United States on Cuba's Bay of Pigs. Since then, the new mayor has leaned noticeably leftward in his awarding of official favors, the citizens complain.

This, then, is Communist activity in Honduras. I have cited it in some detail to reveal how ubiquitous it is—and how it works. To indicate that Honduras is not an isolated case, however, let us look a moment at El Salvador and Guatemala, neighbor nations in Central America, where Castro's major infiltration efforts are being concentrated.

In El Salvador in February 1962 after truly free elections had installed a democratically elected provisional President for the first time in the country's history, the Communists are still active. National Police Director Alnoldo Rodezno announces that posters urging citizens to take violent action against the government were pasted up in San Salvador, Santa Ana, Chalchuapa, Atiquizaya, and Santa Tecla—usually during the night when no one was about. The night of January 24, he says, his men caught several men posting such inflammatory signs. Under rigid questioning, it appeared that they knew little of the meaning of the posters, and were merely paid workers of persons unknown.

And in Guatemala:

June 1960—The government of General Miguel Ydígoras Fuentes announces that the small homemade bombs that have been terrorizing the capital for weeks are the work of Communists. Left-wing non-Communist opponents of the general scoff, pointing out that none of the bombs has hurt anyone, and little property damage has been done—and suggesting that the government set them off itself to "buy sympathy."

But that same month, Mexican Secret Service Chief Javier Orellana declares that he has found and confiscated in Mexico "an enormous cache of arms and ammunition" sent by Cuban Communists via Mexico to their cohorts in Guatemala.

Also in June, the high school students of Guatemala, supported by their teachers, go on strike to protest the firing of a popular left-wing teacher and to demand the resignation of Education Minister Sarbelio Herrera. The strike, extremely well disciplined and organized, is under the direction of known Red agitators, including members of the Teachers' United Front, a Communist-dominated group. And it is opposed, loudly and with more noise than sense, by the Union of Primary School Teachers, whose opposition is so *non sequitur* as to be unworthy of consideration. Never having heard of this latter group, Guatemalan newsmen and government agents seek it out, only to find that it is not listed in the telephone book or city directory and is unknown to any primary schoolteachers in the city. Apparently this was a phantom organization, one of many such formed hastily by the Reds on either side of any issue for their own purposes of agitation.

Hoping to end the strike, Education Minister Herrera resigns. But the strike goes on.

July 1960—Handbills appear throughout Guatemala calling on "the working class" to declare a general strike against the

105

"anti-democratic laws of the clownish government" (anti-Communist Decree 59). Source of the throwaways is the Union of Action and Movement of Railroad Workers (a Communist-dominated group) and the phantom "Organization of Authentic Revolutionary Workers."

Late the same month, fearing general violence, the government declares a state of siege—which means, here, suspension of such constitutional guarantees as the right of free assembly, free speech, and the imposition of early curfews to make policing easier. Even such critics of Ydígoras as Congressman Ernesto Vitori Bertrand, former President of the Congress, admit that the decree is justified and that the emergency is indeed the result of Red activity.

August 1960—Sixty Cuban terrorists were prevented from landing in Guatemala by boat, Ydígoras declares. Despite the fact that terrorist bombs are still exploding, some now with personal injuries, *chapines* laugh—isn't the general really too cute?

The same month, Guatemalan police discover Communist cells in every neighborhood of the capital, each one under the management of a teacher of known Red affiliation.

March 1961—The Guatemalan Congress refuses to extend the anti-Communist laws passed during the regime of Colonel Castillo Armas. Hordes of supporters of former President Jacobo Arbenz, Guatemala's one avowedly Communist chief of state, return here from exile (most of them from Cuba, where they went immediately after the Castro revolution). The remainder of 1961 is suspiciously quiet, leading political observers to predict that more Communist activity is being plotted.

January 1962—Guatemala City's Chief of Police is shot down from a speeding car as he is leaving his home in the capital. President Ydígoras charges a "vast international conspiracy" on the part of the Communists, working through Havana, and again declares a state of siege.

Patterns such as these can be seen in every Latin American country since the Cuban Revolution, even in tiny, ultrademocratic Costa Rica, which is far from a top priority target for

106

the Reds. (They realize, of course, that countries like Costa Rica can be taken by force after the other, easier targets have been secured.)

Toward the end of 1961 a new pattern appears in the Communist line in Latin America—the accent on race and color.

Suddenly, in place of the phrase, "Latin America," such Red-lining papers as *El Cronista* of Honduras switch to the phrases *América morena* (brown America) and *América india*. This, of course, plays on the fact that most of Latin America's people are of mixed extraction and darker skinned than either their own leaders or the average gringo. Playing on this difference, with its concomitant social distinctions, the Communists can create new bitterness here, Alliance for Progress and Peace Corps notwithstanding.

Surveying all of this, one can discern the pattern of Communist activity here—infiltrate, agitate, divide, and conquer. Any opportunity to create discord is taken advantage of; any tactic that disrupts is utilized. The Communists have, of course, a vested interest in instability. Given a sufficiently stressful condition, they can move in, as they did in Cuba. Meanwhile, they can press on the sensitive nerves of nationalism and racism—nerves which we have helped sensitize with our thoughtless arrogance and casual exploitation. Unfortunately, the Communists are past masters of the art of propaganda and far better practical psychologists than we. Furthermore, they are tightly organized and firmly disciplined—what one Commie says in Argentina today will be echoed by another in Mexico tomorrow—while we work quite often at odds with ourselves. But most important, while the Communists have won the confidence of many Latin Americans, we have yet to understand the Latin personality or to make our own personality attractive to Latins.

For example, we still fail to recognize that the dominant political-emotional chord here is anti-officialism; strongly individualistic Latins with the memory of dictatorial government fresh in their minds have yet to adapt to the emerging democracy that they themselves are now creating. Today, in all but four Latin American nations, governments are freely elected.

Thereafter, as any leader here will ruefully explain, they are just as freely criticized, resisted, and, at times, overthrown.

But as we have always done, and are still doing under the Alliance for Progress, we direct our appeal to governments, all but ignoring the people themselves. Meanwhile, the Communists ignore or actively oppose governments, appealing directly to the people.

Leonidas Plaza, Ecuadorean Ambassador to London, put it this way once in a letter to *Time* magazine:

"For Latin Americans in general, Public Enemy Number 1 is the government. . . . The U.S. . . . deals with Latin American republics exclusively through official channels, thus is the direct and basic cause of the 'hate America' epidemic. . . ." (As we have seen, this epidemic has various causes, plain and fancy. Nonetheless Ambassador Plaza's statement pinpoints one major cause.)

When the former American Ambassador to Honduras stuck close to the side of President Villeda Morales in all his travels, intending thereby to manifest U.S.-Honduran solidarity, he earned instead the nickname "the tick," and gave support to the story that the United States supervises everything the Honduran Government does. He was a great friend of the government, but no friend of the people.

Similarly, our "invasion" of the Swan Islands here aroused only a calm and formal protest from the government, but a wrathful howl from the people. Whether these grains of sand in the Caribbean are ours or theirs is unimportant: what matters is that we gave propaganda ammunition to the Communists, drove moderate voices into harmony with the extremists, and made the job tougher for a friendly, democratic leader who, as we have seen, was having troubles enough.

Meanwhile, our Russian competitors remain under cover and avoid such public relations fiascos. After taking over Cuba, they used Cubans as emissaries to the rest of Latin America—tall, bearded soldiers who made friends among their "blood brothers" in the *cantinas* of the poor. Then, attracting young Latin rebels to Havana, they wined, dined, pleased, and flattered them—and

108

indoctrinated them—then sent them home to Honduras, Guatemala, Venezuela, and the rest of the area to act as advance guard for the coming tide of commissars. Where Russians themselves have been in evidence, as in Uruguay and in Mexico, they have uniformly known the language, customs, and psychology of the people well enough to play on them rather than stumble over them.

Of course this apparent brotherhood is cynical; of course the Communists adopt their understanding attitudes as only a means to an end—the enslavement of Latin Americans to the system that has already enslaved the peoples of Poland, Czechoslovakia, and Hungary. But cynical or not, it works—now there is one Red satellite in Latin America and soon there may be more—while our arrogant idealism, in which the adjective is unfortunately more apparent than the noun, has been and is failing.

There are advantages to the sort of cynicism that allows one to tailor history to one's current needs. Since Castro the Red version of Latin American history has undergone a significant change. In 1950 the Soviet Encyclopedia described Simón Bolívar as "opposed to the active participation of the masses in the War of Independence . . . interested only in conserving and perpetuating the Creole feudal system suppressing the peasants. . . . Karl Marx wrote of Bolívar that he tried to convert the Americas into a Federal Republic with himself as dictator." The 1960 version reads, "the grandeur of the Liberator was expressed in his love for the Indian, Negro and peasant, all of whom had risen in arms against the Spanish oppressor. . . . those in our times who criticize Bolívar are themselves either dictators or ideological reactionaries."

Similarly, before Castro, Latin America was not even mentioned in Soviet high school history books; now there is a 227-page Appendix to their *New History of the West*, 197 pages of which are given over entirely to Latin America!

Granted the universality of the laws of thermodynamics, there are inherent advantages to working for disorder instead of order, and these, too, the Communists exploit to the fullest.

109

On November 7, 1960, the 43rd anniversary of the Russian Revolution, Latin America looked like this:

Argentina—Three million union members on strike, paralyzing the country for 24 hours.

Chile—General strike, tying up transportation and commerce.

Brazil—Half a million transportation workers out, shutting down ports and railroads.

(According to Brazilian and Argentine officials, all three strikes were planned and called by the Soviet Embassy in Montevideo, Uruguay.)

Cuba—The island learns officially that it is a "Socialist" state (in the Communist sense of the word).

Uruguay—Officials report the entry of 710 diplomatic pouches from Moscow, weighing over 3 tons. (This is how printed propaganda comes into Latin America, of course.)

El Salvador—Communists exiled under the Lémus regime are now returning in droves as the new junta seeks to adjust itself to governing.

Honduras—Two new parties of the extreme left form, neither officially Communist, both obviously so.

A little over a year later, while sanctions against Castro are being voted at Punta del Este, Uruguay, Latin America looks like this:

Venezuela—Fourteen people are killed in a bus strike that turns into a three-day riot, complete with 50 or more bombs, car burnings and attacks on the U.S. Embassy in Caracas.

Uruguay—Thousands gather in Montevideo shouting "Cuba Sí, Yanquis No"; hundreds march on Punta del Este in an attempt (unsuccessful) to interrupt the meetings.

Guatemala—The capital police chief is shot to death and a new state of siege is declared.

Colombia, Mexico, Peru, Bolivia—Pro-Castro demonstrations are broken up only by tear gas and vigorous police baton clubbing.

Yet when a reporter warns that Communism is on the march in Latin America, official U.S.A. accuses him of sensationalism

110

(the U.S. Embassy in Tegucigalpa wrote me that "there are very, very few pictures of Fidel to be seen in Honduras" after I had reported seeing them from the north coast to the southwest highlands) and unofficial U.S.A.—the public—tends to ignore him. Meanwhile, the march goes on. And for this, the smug diplomats who claim to know Latin America and the complacent citizens who don't care to know it, bear a deep burden of guilt.

But this is as nothing to the guilt they will bear if, through their action or inaction, more of our southern neighbors fall into the clutch of the Communists. By then, however, they will be concerned about their own safety.

And by then it will be too late.

9

The Alliance for Progress

When the Marshall Plan of aid to Europe was beginning, its founder, General George C. Marshall, told Latin Americans that they were not eligible for such aid since their area was of less than strategic importance to the United States. A decade and a half later, on August 16, 1961, the Alliance for Progress was launched—an aid plan for Latin America alongside of which the Marshall Plan looks a little like the Salvation Army coffee-and-doughnuts program.

Under the Alliance for Progress, Latin America will receive $2 billion a year for 10 years, or a total of $20 billion. This economic transfusion is to be used for ten major programs:

1. Economic growth of at least 2.5 per cent a year for each country;
2. Broadening the economic base of all one-crop economies;
3. More realistic distribution of national wealth;
4. Six years of schooling for every child;
5. More rapid industrialization;
6. Increased farm production;
7. Better health programs;
8. Low cost housing;
9. Price stabilization for basic exports such as coffee;
10. Establishment of "common markets."

Although headlines here and Stateside streamered the $20 billion, two aspects of the Alliance for Progress were even more newsworthy: a new posture on our part toward several signifi-

112

cant social problems here; and a new concept of aid, under which the recipient must first meet several conditions of a social as well as an economic nature.

Previously, we had believed, or acted as if we believed, that development of Latin America could be left to private enterprise, even though the capital so furnished was more often exploitation money than development capital. Now Latin America was to come under our foreign aid program supported by public funds, in a big way.

Earlier, we had refused to discuss price controls on Latin American commodities; now we were ready to implement them.

Previously, we would grant no loans to government-controlled monopolies; now we would extend funds even to the oil monopolies, Pemex in Mexico and Petrobras in Brazil.

Before, we scrupulously avoided helping land reform; now we were insisting on it as a condition before aid would be granted.

This is only one phase of the new dedication to social change represented by the Alliance for Progress; whereas we had earlier demanded only that inflation be halted and a favorable climate for foreign investment be created, now we were calling for improvements in local systems of taxation and land tenure, health, education, and housing. In other words, while our earlier aid to Latin America was limited in vision as well as in dollars, the Alliance represented a multi-billion dollar bonanza and a new accent on social liberalization.

Yet within a few months after the program was announced, the criticism started anew, and various Latin American governments were seeking their slices of the big melon aside from the provisions of the over-all plan. Can it be, as such papers as *The Miami Herald* would have it, that we are bound to be criticized just because we are a rich uncle? Are Latins inveterate gripers, unappreciative of a helping hand, as *Life* magazine believes? Or are there weaknesses in the Alliance that dull even the golden glitter of $20 billion?

Probably a little of all this. Rich uncles are always subject to criticism, although some distribute largesse with commendable grace; anti-Yanqui feeling is, by now, a habit here; and there are signal weaknesses in the Alliance for Progress.

The major hope of the Alliance for Progress, in its objective of developing Latin America, lies in more rapid industrialization. In this sense, our newest aid scheme for these hungry nations differs little from previous plans or from the alternate programs that were adduced while the *alianza* was being hammered out. It is natural that a society grown rich on industry will see potential riches for other societies in similar development. But for many Latin leaders, especially the intellectuals of the left, industrialization has many—perhaps too many—inherent disadvantages for their countries.

Perhaps two thirds of Latin America's people today earn their living from the land. Agricultural production has increased at a slow rate in recent years and has actually decreased in some cases, despite various technical aid programs. To a poor man, food is the biggest part of his total expense—and if food is not available locally, it costs even more. The accent on industrialization inevitably implies a secondary emphasis on agriculture. And the new wealth derived from industrialization inevitably accrues, not to the two thirds who are farmers, but to the one third who are not. It is, in fact, quite likely that increased industrial wealth also means greater relative poverty for the majority. For example, the $90-a-week wage of the Chilean copper miner so overwhelms the dollar-a-day of the rural worker that the latter has less ability than before to compete economically—or even to survive. Living costs in Chile have risen 50 per cent in the last 3 years; industrial workers can at least attempt to tag after this rise with wage increases, but for the rural worker there is no such aid.

Mexico is more highly industrialized than Chile and the other Latin American countries, and in Mexico the picture is confirmed again. According to Señora Ifegenia Navarrete, a leading Mexican economist, industrialization in her country between 1950 and 1957 made the rich richer and the poor even poorer. She points out that over-all family incomes rose 23 per cent in this period. However, the incomes of the bottom one fifth of

Mexico's families dropped nearly 2 per cent while the next lowest third barely managed to maintain their earning level. Gross national product rose almost 50 per cent in 7 years—but the top families, a mere 5 per cent of the population, skimmed off 37 per cent of all this.[1]

It is easier, and politically safer, to plan a new industrial city than to tackle the age-old problems of a land tenure system based on privilege. Former President Kubitschek's Brasilia, bold and beautiful as it was, cost less time, effort, money—and political risk—than a march into the jungles where lie the agricultural frontiers. But taking the easy way means leaving untouched the basic problems, thereby creating an ever more dissatisfied, dissident mass, a mass that is a pushover for the Communists.

As Arnold Toynbee has pointed out, communism itself is a Western creation, growing out of the discontents of an industrialized society. Its creators were "brought up in the Rhineland and spent the best part of their working lives in London and in Manchester respectively. . . . There was nothing in the Russian tradition that could have led the Russians to invent communism for themselves; and it is certain that they would never have dreamed of it had it not been lying, ready-made, there in the West."[2]

There is, I think, an inherent conflict in the Alliance's search for democracy through industrialization. As Marston Bates has indicated, Japan transformed itself into an industrial society with little imported capital and few imported experts—by means of "a tight, autocratic control of the economy by a group of people who were determined to carry through with the industrialization process, and who were able to dictate and control the required measures. This is hardly in accord with the principles of democracy, and presents . . . a real dilemma to those Westerners who want to remake the world in accordance with both democratic and industrial ideas at the same time."[3]

[1] Ifigenia Navarrete, *Income Distribution and Economic Development of Mexico,"* Mexico, 1960.

[2] Arnold Toynbee, op. cit.   [3] Marston Bates, op. cit.

In Central America, El Salvador presents a similar example. It is the area's most highly industrialized and most financially stable republic. It got that way through the tight control of the famous Fourteen Families, whose rapid development of industry has worsened rather than bettered the condition of the rural majority.

The economic imbalances of industrialization are only part of its evils. With industrialization come problems of rapid urban growth and rural decline, of slums and increased juvenile delinquency, of air and stream pollution, of nervous tension, heart disease, neurosis, and psychosis. Industrialized man, although he may have more money in his pocket, is, by definition, organized man—man subjugated to the herd and to the machine. The Latin personality, more fiercely independent than that of northerly peoples, resents such pressures. (See, for example, the work of the Mexican painters, especially Siqueiros, whose theme is man devoured by the machine.)

The cultural orientation of tropical peoples, Latins included, is emotional and humanistic rather than mechanistic. Even their languages are so oriented, making technical concepts difficult to express, while emotional ones flow with a precision, richness, and economy that no northern tongue can match. (Our "starter" takes three words in Spanish—*"motor de arranque"*; their *"simpático"* is not exactly translated by "sympathetic, charming, likable, or nice.") Pointing out that no tropical region has yet developed an industrial economy, Bates attributes it to this cultural factor, noting that "the reorientation of the cultural pattern (which would include political and social systems) will be no simple task, either for outsiders or for local governing groups."[4]

The Alliance faces another problem of staggering proportions—population growth in Latin America.[5] Every year, for every thousand workers here, workers whose take-home pay

4 Op. cit., p. 230.
5 Much of the material on population that follows is derived from various publications of the Population Reference Bureau, Washington, D.C.

116

averages less than a dollar a day, 15 male school children are ready to start their education. Contrast this with a country like England, whose workers are paid ten times as much, and every thousand of whom must pay annually for the education of only one male child. In other words, the burden of education in largely illiterate Latin America is 150 times greater than in almost completely literate Great Britain. This is the numbers game of population growth translated into human terms. So translated, it represents the major problem of development here. And this is the problem that no government in the hemisphere has yet made a move to tackle, including ours under the Alliance for Progress.

The Alliance aims for an economic growth rate of at least 2.5 per cent in every Latin American country; should it achieve this aim, the gains would be more than absorbed by population increases in every country except Argentina, Bolivia, Colombia, and Uruguay, the only Latin republics with a rate of population growth below 2.5 per cent.

This is the fastest-growing major area in the world; every year, over 5,000,000 hungry new mouths are added to the already hungry population; in less than 30 years, the population will be twice what it is today. Under such phenomenal growth rates, the investment of $20 billion can, at best, achieve no more than equilibrium: for every forward step in health, education, and welfare, for every new factory, for every gain in agricultural production, millions of new dependents will appear to absorb the increase.

There is precedent for this gloomy prophecy in the case of India. There, "per capita income has gone up slightly—to around $65 a year after thirteen years of independence and two five-year plans. During that time, some $22 billion of development capital has been invested. Population soars at a fairly constant rate of close to 2 per cent, which all but obliterates the increase in production of goods and food."[6] Note that India has received $2 billion more than is slated for Latin America

[6] Rowland Evans, Jr., "India Experiments with Sterilization," *Harper's*, November 1961.

under the *alianza,* and that India's population growth rate is 0.6 per cent less than that here.

Many writers have called the Alliance for Progress a Marshall Plan for Latin America; indeed, I may have implied something of the sort in the beginning of this chapter. I hasten to correct that impression, with its implication that a program effective in Western Europe can be equally effective here. Western Europe is an area of low population growth, although its population density is high. Western Europe has many more people in the productive ages of 15 to 65 than in the dependent ages below 15 and above 65. Eighty million of Latin America's 200 million people are in the dependent age groups. Western Europe's people are almost universally literate, while the majority in Latin America are not; they have longstanding technological skills that are still rare here. And, of course, aiding Western Europe meant rebuilding the pre-existing industrial complexes in the Ruhr, the Saar, and Great Britain; aiding Latin America means creating such vast installations from scratch, a nearly hopeless task under the best of circumstances.

The most significant difference, however, is in population growth. In Western Europe, production gains benefited a relatively stable number of people; here they will be absorbed by a rapidly increasing number of people. Furthermore, there is now in Latin America a huge and ever-expanding backlog of young people entering the reproductive ages. Assuming that current high birth rates continue, over-all population increase will accelerate. In so doing, it will provide even more young people who spend fifteen dependent years and then leap into reproduction to create two or more new dependents to offset their single contribution to production.

How did Latin America become such a fertile area? It began with the necessity to create new people based on the extremely high death rates and early death ages of the 17th through the 19th centuries. But with the advent of simple sanitation measures and effective insecticides, death rates were reduced sharply almost overnight. And with this reduction, high birth rates

118

became obsolete—yet the tradition remained, with no sign of abatement. Public health programs have been cutting the death rate since the 1920's. Such programs did not seriously affect other underdeveloped areas until 1946. Thus Latin America has much lower death rates today than most of Africa and Asia—and concomitantly higher rates of population growth, making the problems of development here actually more difficult than they are in less-ready-for-development Africa and Asia.

Unless one wants to contemplate a new increase in the death rate as a means of limiting population growth here, the only possible solution lies in decreasing the birth rate. Yet no Latin American government has put forth any population program, and the United States remains silent on the problem—as well it might, considering the probable reactions of Latins if we tried to tell them how to do this, too.

Many students of the area, including local political leaders, have attempted to minimize the problem by pointing to certain vast underpopulated areas, such as the interiors of Ecuador and Venezuela and Brazil's Amazon Basin. Yet even with these potential farm and home sites, Ecuador has only 1.1 arable acres per capita, Venezuela 0.7, and Brazil 0.9. Compare these figures, for countries that are primarily agricultural, with the 2.9 arable acres per capita of North America, which is primarily industrial. Most Latin American countries have fewer arable acres per capita than the world average of 1.2; only Argentina has more (4.0) than the United States and Canada.[7] In the face of these figures, it is difficult indeed to understand the statement of Felipe Herrera, Director of the Inter-American Development Bank, when he claims that the real problem is "the distribution of people on the land and not the distribution of land among people," unless one credits high soil fertility and the ability to produce crops year-round in tropical areas with a vaster potential than has ever been realized. (One must grant, however, that these are potent factors—tropical America is capable of living entirely from agricultural production if the population does not expand too rapidly, as it is now.)

[7] United Nations *Demographic Yearbook,* 1959.

119

Obviously, the lagging agricultural production of a number of countries here could and should be boosted by technical improvements (yield per acre is still pitifully low) and by marching into virgin areas and utilizing the fertile soil that is now going to waste. Brazil's Amazon Basin, for example, constitutes almost 5 per cent of the world's land surface, and remains untouched. But what a formidable problem this development would be, with its necessity for clearing thick, dangerous jungle, for relocating tens of thousands of families, for shipping into the interior the seeds, the implements, and other materials that go to make up a farm! And meanwhile, the population will go on swelling. . . .

The simple statistical truth of the matter is that sheer numbers stand in the way of social and economic progress here. Latin America's impoverished workers do not have the wherewithal to educate their children; under the rosiest predictions of what the Alliance for Progress would accomplish, they will still not have it. Lagging education means continuing ignorance and illiteracy; these factors in themselves contribute to higher birth rates, since educated people gravitate toward limiting their families while uneducated people don't; the vicious cycle continues.

Just because so many here are uneducated, there is little hope that there ever will be any grass-roots movement to cut the birth rate by any means. Highly literate Argentina and Uruguay have the area's lowest birth rates (but almost equally literate Costa Rica has a very high one, testifying to the fact that education alone will not automatically solve the problem).

There are other pressures that tend to maintain the traditional pattern of early and high reproduction. One is Catholicism (although the church opposes only certain methods of birth control and the *indicazione* specifically permits it under medical, eugenic, economic, and social exigencies—and although Poland, one of the world's most Catholic nations, has legalized abortions). Another is the Indian tradition. Among the Lencas of Honduras and El Salvador, and among numerous other more southerly tribes, the entire approach to marriage is one of enabling the early and rapid having of children. The suitor "borrows" the girl he sets his cap for from her parents for six months; if, in that time, she has not become pregnant, he looks for another girl. Indeed, the tradition is so well preserved that the Indians see no conflict between it and their nominal Catholicism. I grin every time I remember the rueful look a local priest had as he told me about the Indian who had asked him for the "loan" of the girl who was his ward!

The Spanish sex code—the one they practice as revealed in life and literature—also militates against the success of any birth control program. To a Spanish woman, sterility is the worst possible curse: she wants a son to continue the line and to have handy in case revenge against some outside offender is required at a later date. The accent on childbearing comes from Catholicism; that on continuing the line and on revenge comes from the Moors, who left their mark on Spain and her American colonies in more than architecture alone.

Finally, there is the phenomenon that is peculiarly Latin American—the cult of the male (*el culto del machismo*). This, too, is a force against birth control. A man is not a man until he has children, and those children had better be sons, not daughters. Thus he proves his masculinity; and thus, he teaches his sons, must they prove theirs. The male child is pampered throughout infancy and prized much more highly than the female. When, in childhood and adolescence, he gets into any kind of trouble, his father tends to defend him: "He's a *macho*, isn't he?" Perhaps it is universally true that in school girls are better behaved than boys, but based on experience teaching here and in the States, I can testify that "boys will be boys" has considerably more pungency in Latin America.

In 1959 a presidential committee on foreign aid recommended that the United States should help the hungry nations set up birth control programs. But in the election campaigns that followed, every major candidate adopted a stand against such a program. Part of the hesitancy is dictated by good taste and a sound sense of public relations; another part by that wide streak

121

of prudishness that runs through our society (a prudishness, incidentally, which is another item on the checklist of things Latins don't much like about us).

If the people of Latin America will not voluntarily limit their fertility, if the government of the United States cannot and should not even discuss the subject, the burden falls on the individual governments here. To date, it is a burden they have refused to shoulder; the cold statistics indicate that this refusal has already interfered with the very social and economic programs they most vociferously espouse, and will, in the near future, make the success of such programs literally impossible.

Beset by internal political strife typical of any emerging democracy, threatened by Communist infiltration and agitation, fighting for their political lives, it is no wonder that Latin leaders have scrupulously avoided even mentioning a topic so counter to the normal rhythms of their peoples as birth control: one word on the subject could well mean the overthrow of a government and the end of other carefully prepared advances.

But until solid local government pressure arouses an awareness in Latin Americans that they are breeding themselves into starvation, the numbers game will go on, and the ritual of reproduction will prove to be a dance of death.

Insofar as the position of the United States is concerned, it is high time we, too, faced facts, even if they be sexual in nature, and followed the recommendations of the Third Interim Report, July 13, 1959, of the President's Committee to Study the U.S. Military Assistance Program:

"That, in order to meet more effectively the problems of economic development, the United States assist those countries with which it is cooperating in economic aid programs, *on request* [italics mine] in the formulation of their plans designed to deal with the problem of rapid population growth. . . ."

It is not incumbent on us, nor would it be seemly for us, to urge changes in reproductive habits of other peoples. But we should stand ready to provide money and information for such changes *when they are asked for* by one or another government here. The mere fact of such readiness might help leaders

122

here move toward programs of birth control, without which the Alliance has little chance of success.

Albert O. Hirschman points out some of the internal weaknesses of the Alliance in an article in *The Reporter:* "How," he asks, "shall we judge whether a country is taking sufficiently bold steps in the direction of social justice to be entitled to aid? Obviously we have neither the intellectual tools nor the time to undertake such evaluations; we will have to be content with the more modest goal of enhancing the attention that the governments of Latin America are giving to the main causes of discontent in their countries. . . . Thus we may have a dilemma: if a country has the will to improve the condition of its lower classes, the proffered funds may not be needed, while if such a determination is lacking, the offer of funds will not in itself create it." (I disagree with Professor Hirschman on this latter point. There is no Latin American country which could not use financial help. And in any given country, whose "will" shall we consider—the will of the President, of the Congress, of the rich, of the poor? Almost uniformly, the President and the poor are determined to improve the condition of the lower classes; almost uniformly, they have been stymied by the other two.)

Probing more deeply, Professor Hirschman points out that the prevailing mood here of intellectuals and policymakers, whether in or out of office, is one which seeks no alliances whatsoever, with us or with the Russians; Latin Americans want to chart their own course. Given this mood, he points out, "the whole idea of a new alliance . . . may not strike the right tone. . . . In other words, we may well have to choose between *alianza* and *progreso*."[8]

He is seconded here by the Whaley-Eaton Foreign Letter (No. 25, 1961), which reports that leaders in Latin America want an aid program "with no political or economic strings attached." They feel that they are capable of diagnosing their own social and economic ills; that they should make the decisions as to what remedies should be applied; that anything else directly

[8] Albert O. Hirschman, "Second Thoughts on the Alliance for Progress," *The Reporter*, May 25, 1961.

123

interferes with the "sovereignty and autodetermination" of their countries.

Yet much of our uncontrolled aid in the past has been wasted. I think of our school lunch program in Peru for 30,000 children in the highlands. A small thing compared with the Alliance— and yet a school lunch in such areas of chronic semistarvation is often the only decent meal a child gets all day. Two months after we had offered food and distribution facilities, the Peruvian Government had not taken any effective action to utilize them, nor had it put up the $15,000 needed to pay inland transportation from the ports to the highlands. Also in Peru, a year after we had granted several millions for housing and for agricultural programs related to land reform, acceptance by the Congress was still not forthcoming. (Some *diputados* were against the programs because of economic interest of the groups they represent; others wanted them delayed until after the June 1962 elections so that these successes could not be used by Premier Beltrán in a bid for the Presidency.) Similar examples have occurred in every country, where vested interests, politics, or government inefficiency have stymied our aid efforts.

The real dilemma, then, is this—uncontrolled aid often does not reach the people we want to help, yet any attempt to control aid arouses resentment on the part of everybody. The Alliance for Progress, with its careful criteria for aid eligibility, hangs on the second horn of the dilemma. But could it do otherwise?

Given the time at which the program was hammered out and the motivations for extending it then, and in the way we did, the answer is No: we were damned if we did and damned if we didn't. As Professor Hirschman also points out in the article just cited, "Castro's rise to power made the United States favor a more intensive use of public funds as a principal instrument of foreign policy . . . if a new Cuba was to be prevented in Latin America, every effort should be made to correct similar faults and prevent similar grievances." (Fidel himself paraphrased this more simply and forcefully when he told Latin America that the $20 billion *alianza* was his gift to them. Many people here believe him—and with some justification.)

124

Before Castro ever came into power in Cuba, foresighted Latin American leaders like Colombia's President Alberto Lleras Camargo and Costa Rica's José Figueres were warning the United States that we must act big and fast if this part of the world was to be saved from stronger than ever anti-Yanqui feelings and pro-Communist leanings. Vice President Nixon was stoned and spat upon in Venezuela; the brother of former President Eisenhower reported in 1953 and again in 1958 that time was running out. Yet we waited; it is highly possible that we waited too long.

Given our past history of economic domination and military intervention in Latin America; given our negative attitude toward the area as expressed by General Marshall and others; given our arrogant behavior here as detailed in the first part of this book, it would have been difficult for any new aid scheme to have won favor among Latins. But given, on top of all this, the crisis, for us, of Red penetration into "our" hemisphere, our reaction in terms of overdue help could never pass for generosity and our insistence that that help be accepted on our terms could never be seen by Latins as anything but further intervention in their internal affairs for our own good.

We are novices at the game of changing what goes on inside another country and subject to the fumbles of amateurs. We fail to recognize, for example, that the left-wing groups most ardent for land reform have also been those most bitterly anti-United States. How will they reconcile their problem now that our policy has switched? It is likely that they will continue to be against us, and drop the push for land reform, now tainted by our support. There are hints that exactly this is happening now in several countries. In a more general sense, those revolutionary groups most in favor of social reform of all kinds have also been the groups we opposed in the past; could not our espousal of a large part of their cause motivate them to seek another cause in order to remain anti-Yanqui?

Finally, there is the unfortunate fact that demanding compliance with certain rules before aid money will be granted does not automatically guarantee compliance, even where the chief executive of some nation sincerely hopes to provide it. Land reform, for example, is, as of this writing, neatly pigeon-holed in committee in the congresses of Peru and Colombia; income tax legislation in Guatemala is in a similar position. Shall we withhold promised funds because these legislative bodies have frustrated the desires of their Presidents, or shall we grant the aid despite noncompliance "because the presidents tried"? And what is to prevent a president from claiming that he tried when he knew all along that certain legislation introduced by him had no chance of passing?

These, of course, are political subtleties, and Fulano de Tal (the Latin-American John Doe) is not concerned with them when he reacts negatively to our latest plans for his uplift. What he sees is our motivation, our real purpose, and this is what he resents.

Ever since the Good Neighbor Policy was buried with its creator, we have treated Latin America as a poor and unwanted relation. Suddenly, under the threat of Communist gains, we see it as a black sheep we must paint white at all costs, lest it change to red. Latins recognize our newest and most openhanded policy as one of political expediency first and of friendship second. It is obvious to them that our new-found concern for social reform here stems from belated recognition that lack of such change helped cause Cuba to fall into Red hands; that our sudden interest in land reform, diametrically opposed to past policy, is similarly motivated; that the condition of the people here is only of concern to us now insofar as it represents a threat to our own security in the hemisphere. On these terms, our demands for social reform appear no different, at heart, than our earlier demands for an inflation-free economy that would protect our investment in Latin America.

In the Alliance for Progress, we have finally put our money where our mouth is—but not where our heart is. We really do not care what happens to Latin Americans as people; they are only pawns in the game of power politics. Our extractive industries are still here to exploit the soil and subsoil riches of the area; a large part of our aid still goes to the military, who represent a force for democracy in only a handful of countries, a repressive force in the rest; we still maintain our legal right to such contested territories as the Panama Canal and the Honduran Swan Islands; we still formulate plans of economic benefit to us that injure our southern neighbors, such as the recently announced scheme to unload our stockpiled tin in order to drive down the price, which Bolivia sees as "an act of real economic aggression."

Worse, we are using the Alliance for Progress as a blunt instrument to enforce compliance with our wishes in Latin America. When it began to appear, at the Punta del Este meeting in January 1962, that we would not secure the votes we needed for strong action against Castro, Secretary of State Dean Rusk used some gentle blackmail: "Security from extracontinental intervention is essential to the success of our cooperative efforts to achieve social and economic advancement under the Alliance for Progress." And several Congressmen, with or without Dean Rusk's knowledge and approval, lobbied furiously, one going so far as to say, "Things will be disagreeable in Congress" if Cuba is not strongly censured.

In the final chapter I will present a plan for eliminating these obstacles to a real rapprochement between the United States and Latin America, based on the Alliance for Progress as it stands plus several additional steps that should have been taken first but that, coming later, might still salvage our reputation in this part of the world. But I must restate here that no plan can work as long as the motives behind it are questionable—Latin Americans will not like us as people until we are likable.

As Juan Milla Bermúdez, Honduran Minister of Communications and Public Works, put it to me recently:

"The problems of U.S.-Latin American relations could resolve themselves with relative ease if the flow of economic aid, so necessary to our precarious economies, had added to it and mixed with it a similar flow of authentic good will and comprehension."

10

The Peace Corps

Even more than the Alliance for Progress, President Kennedy's Peace Corps captured the imagination of people around the world. Stateside, volunteers for this virtually unpaid group of world-wide hard workers streamed in at the rate of 100 a day; from dozens of countries came requests for Peace Corpsmen to launch literally hundreds of projects. And the Communists, predictably, called them "spies."

Here in Latin America, press commendation of the program echoed that of the States: it was "grass roots diplomacy," "Christianity in practise"; the Corpsmen were "bright, dedicated, non-materialistic, true workers for peace."

Amid all the hoopla, few people bothered to examine the program with any real care; concentrating on the unquestionable ideological appeal of the basic idea, national writers who might have been analytical were, instead, eulogistic. Stateside, the local press confined itself to local angles ("Anybody here from Pa.?") from which readers could derive a sense of identification with this newest missionary venture.

What is the Peace Corps and what is it supposed to achieve? Who are the Corpsmen; what is their training; what can they be expected to accomplish?

President Kennedy's Executive Order establishing the Corps said this: "The vast task of economic development urgently requires skilled people to do the work of society—to help teach in the schools, construct development projects, demonstrate modern methods of sanitation in the villages, and perform a hundred other tasks . . ."

Later listing of the sort of assignments Corpsmen would draw included "well drilling, laying water and sewage pipe lines, supervising . . . gardens . . . building sanitary latrines . . ."

Volunteers for these assignments include teachers, mathematicians, anthropologists, philosophers, geologists, engineers, linguists—all trained specialists, most of them recent college graduates in their early twenties. Bright, eager young men and women almost uniformly dedicated to "doing something personal for peace."

In the absence of more specific objectives than those laid out in the original Executive Order and expanded in the later detailing of work assignments, the first criticism of the Peace Corps arose: why mathematicians and philosophers to build sanitary latrines; couldn't an African or a Bolivian with some special training do the same thing? The second major criticism came from Federal workers in the old ICA and similar agencies, who complained that Peace Corps projects duplicated some of their work and could be expected, in many cases, to interfere rather than help.

Perhaps the most significant analysis of all was made by Professor Benjamin DeMott, writing in *Harper's* (September 1961) on "The Peace Corps' Secret Mission." Serving more as clarification of the fuzzy program than as critique, Professor DeMott's article answers, at least in part, the two criticisms noted above. Unfortunately, it raises even graver doubts about the outcome of the imaginative venture known as the Peace Corps.

Citing a "new, almost completely unpublicized theory of Foreign Aid," Professor DeMott explains that "the best hope of the West lies in the possibility of transforming masses of rural folk—people long afflicted by a sense of total powerlessness—into men conscious of a capacity to alter their lives by alert public action." In order to do this, he explains, Peace Corpsmen will not offer condescending lectures on citizenship—instead, they will "find a vital local project that can serve as a laboratory." Beginning by talking with local people and learning from them what project stirs their imagination, the Peace

129

Corpsmen helps draw them together "as a group conscious of itself" and lets them move toward community action aimed at a specific positive end, whether that end be a new rural school or a village latrine. Throughout, "he has clearly in mind that his final purposes are to shape community attitudes, to encourage habits of community decision and representative action, and to develop understanding of the idea of elective authority." Noting that Peace Corpsmen have not been informed of this (and thereby so informing them), Professor DeMott concludes, "their true task is that of showing forth the one Americanism that can be shared instead of envied . . . their true success would be to leave behind the one kind of installation that can be counted on to rebuild itself."

Along the line, Professor DeMott complains about the lack of indoctrination of Corpsmen in their "secret mission"; because of this lack, he considers that they do not know their jobs and may well be expected to fail.

The truth is, however, that their training is lacking at a more basic level—that of familiarity with the language and customs of the countries in which they will serve. True, they work 60 hours a week on a 6-day schedule, learning these things (plus U.S. culture, how to ride a mule, soccer, etc.). But they are on an average 8-week program, out of which they can only hope to acquire smatterings of the needed information and insight. (I recall the U.S. Army program in Japanese during World War II in which I participated: 60 hours a week for a year, at the end of which only a handful of students spoke fluent Japanese and none was really prepared to live in Japan as anything except a beginner.)

I remember a conversation with the military commander of the Honduran Department of Intibucá, Captain Moisés Sánchez. "I was born in Danlí," the captain told me, "and I served mainly in the capital. When I came here to Intibucá it was like coming to another country. The customs, the attitudes, even the language was different. Frankly, I worked through my executive officer for a full year before I started dealing directly with the people; I wanted to understand them, make myself understood

130

to them, without any unfortunate errors. Now I get along like one of them, and I think our relations with the public are as good as any post in the country." (They are, indeed, which is something of an achievement, considering the rash of armed clashes between the military and the civil guard in Honduras in recent years.)

A little hesitantly, so as not to offend, the captain continued. "Frankly," he said again, "I can't understand how your *Cuerpo de Paz* can hope to achieve much. Most of them are youngsters without experience and almost none of them really know the language or the people of the countries they are going to. I hope they don't get into too much trouble. . . ."

It was, I remember, a week after that chat that 1,000 university students in Nigeria adopted a resolution demanding the withdrawal of Peace Corps members from their country because of one girl's plaint about "primitive living conditions." The girl, one of 37 volunteers in training at the University College of Ibadan, had sent a postcard to a friend in Massachusetts. Somehow the card had been lost and was found on the campus. It read, in part: "With all the training we have had we were really not prepared for the squalor and absolutely primitive living conditions rampant both in the cities and in the bush. . . . Everyone except us lives in the streets, cooks in the streets and even goes to bathroom in the streets."

Following the protest, the young woman apologized to college authorities and resigned from her post (she is now working in Peace Corps headquarters in Washington). She did not explain how her training could have left her as unprepared for life in Nigeria as she apparently was, or how her innocence could have allowed her to write such uncomplimentary reactions on a postcard, which is often an open letter, as this one turned out to be.

There is little doubt that the violent reaction of Nigerians was fanned by Communists, who seem to be everywhere, and always ready to make the most of any error on our part. The point is that they will inevitably find more errors to exploit when we are represented by the young, inexperienced people

131

the Peace Corps almost uniformly recruits. Better by far to have followed the advice of W. R. Grace, who called for a "Senior Specialist Corps" made up of those highly qualified men and women with years of foreign service who retire annually from industry and government.

But none of this touches the core of the probable new disaster for the United States that the Peace Corps represents, namely, the spadework that it will perform for the Communists. Peace Corps assignments are for two years. In that time, the Corpsman must come to know more of the country in which he serves, its language and customs, than he could have learned in his short training period; must interview local people and find out what projects interest them; must show them how to set out to achieve their aims, teach them strange new methods of democratic representation, guide them to district, state, or national authorities who can, perhaps, supply needed materials; must show them the engineering basics of the job, whatever they may be—and then, before, at, or shortly after the time of achievement, must move on.

Leaving behind him a newly aroused rural group, organized for action for the first time and feeling its unaccustomed power, casting around for a direction to move in, a new outlet for its young, lusty energies.

And here the Communists step in. Past masters at the art of exploiting innocent citizens in other countries (see, for example, what happened in Monjarás with the peasants seeking parcels of land, Chapter 8), they easily take over the groups we so painfully brought into being. And within weeks, community action has become communal action; democracy has become "socialism"; the "installation that can be counted on to rebuild itself" has become, instead, a self-perpetuating monster.

Home again, our idealistic Peace Corpsman is lecturing to Rotary and Lions about life in far-off Chile or Bolivia, and accepting warm congratulations on his achievement.

11

Latin America Today

As this is written, Cuba has quit the Organization of American States "one jump ahead of the sheriff," and our newspapers, magazines, and wire services are celebrating a victory for the United States and a rout for the Communists in the Western Hemisphere.

That victory is more Pyrrhic than empiric.

To begin with, the members of the OAS voted to oust Cuba from the organization, but not to apply individual diplomatic or economic sanctions against the Castro regime. Thus the OAS no more than officially confirmed what had obviously long existed—the withdrawal of Cuba from the inter-American system. To the Castro regime, which already had more ties with Russia and her satellites than with the Western Hemisphere nations, this decision came as no more than a symbolic slap on the wrist. But to the remainder of the American community, it came as an unfortunately timed hope that Communism was being contained here, a hope that is already allowing many Americans, north and south, to lapse into their usual complacency.

Secondly, although 19 of the Latin American members of OAS agreed with the United States that the Castro regime is Communist and therefore incompatible with the democratic system of this hemisphere, only 13 of them voted with the United States to do anything about it. These 13 nations have a population of 55,000,000—in comparison with the 140,000,000 of the six large nations[1] that abstained from voting to oust Cuba

[1] Brazil, Mexico, Argentina, Chile, Bolivia, and Ecuador.

133

from the OAS. In the words of one foreign minister, Cuba was expelled "by getting a majority of pygmies to outvote a minority of giants."

Thirdly, the necessary majority was achieved only by diplomatic blackmail on our part: we threatened that funds from the Alliance for Progress might not be forthcoming unless some action was taken against the Castro regime.

In sum, the Punta del Este Conference, although it did result in the declarations that Cuba is a Communist satellite and that communism is incompatible with the American system, was no signal victory either for the United States or for democracy.

Following that widely misinterpreted meeting came two announcements from Brazil that led to further misunderstanding: that "Che" Guevara's guerrilla warfare handbook had been declared contraband, and that President João Goulart would soon visit the United States. Our press responded with joyful speculation that the most neutralist of the Latin nations was now leaning away from the Communists and toward us.

But most of the damage that can be done by the guerrilla warfare pamphlet has already been done, and declaring it contraband in no way offsets this. And Brazil, under Goulart, led the six nations that opposed any action against Castro. (It would have done the same under Goulart's predecessor, Jânio Quadros, also no great friend of the United States.)

Yet, even as Guevara's treatise was being belatedly outlawed, and Brazil's chief of state was looking opportunistically northward, Brazil was reaffirming, in the OAS Council, the decision she had made long before the Punta del Este meeting— not to intervene in Cuba in any way.

It is evident that the apparent softening toward the United States on Brazil's part is no more than casting tortillas upon the waters in the hope they will come back white bread, neatly wrapped in wax paper clearly marked "Alliance for Progress: $20,000,000,000."

Just as it is obvious, from bombings, burnings, and killings in Venezuela, Uruguay, Colombia, Peru, Bolivia, Mexico, and

134

Guatemala during the Punta del Este meetings, that Castro can still count on friends among the people here, no matter what their governments may do.

Less obvious, however, is the fact that the Communist beachhead is now firmly established in this hemisphere. Latin America today is thoroughly infiltrated with Havana-trained Red agents who will continue their work of subversion and agitation *whether Castro falls or not.* As of this writing, an estimated 2,500 Latin American lawyers, labor leaders, student organizers, and others have been put through the Havana indoctrination mill, returning to their native countries to work toward the coming tide of commissars; literally thousands of tons of printed propaganda have been distributed throughout the area; hundreds of tons of small to medium arms have been handed out to trigger-happy workers, students, and *campesinos.* The overthrow of Castro—or, better said, of the Communist regime which he currently heads—would cut down the intensity of this subversive flow, but would in no way offset the damage that has already been done. Nor can the Alliance for Progress, the Peace Corps, or routine diplomacy as now practiced effectively curtail the activities of the Communists.

The brutal fact is that communism is winning successive small battles in the Cold War in the Western Hemisphere, and will continue to do so in the near future regardless of events in Cuba. Meanwhile, the upcoming Latin leaders who recognize that fact—Peru's Haya de la Torre, Mexico's López Mateos, and Brazil's Goulart—are following neutralist policies to assure them of permanency and their countries of progress under the new Latin American mood.

Still inchoate and ill defined, this mood nonetheless presents certain clear-cut facets:

Unionist among the Latin American sister republics;
Neutralist as between the United States and Russia;
Opportunist toward the world at large.

Put another way, today's liberals in Latin America see their own political future and that of their peoples in *trade* with any country from which they can gain advantage (including Russia and Red China; see Chapter 2) but in *treaties* only among themselves. They recognize that Communist agitators in their own ranks will have their scalps if they swing too far toward the United States; that funds from us will be slow in coming if they swing too far toward Russia; that in union among themselves, coupled with international political neutralism, lies their true advantage. And who knows? Russia and the United States may soon destroy each other, leaving the Latin American bloc the most potent in the world. . . .

(Furthermore, they recognize that the continued existence of a Communist regime just 90 miles from the United States forces our official attention southward, and impels us to pursue a moderate, yet openhanded, policy. Why should they drive out Fidel —the goose who caused the United States to lay a golden egg?)

Such Machiavellian reasoning on the part of a single national leader here, even though he is a leader of a large country, might have little practical meaning. But when it is shared by several such leaders, it begins to assume real geopolitical importance. And when those leaders are also astute enough to maneuver their nationalistic countries toward new-found unity, neutralism in Latin America acquires a pragmatic significance equal to that anywhere in today's world.

The pattern of closer ties among sister nations is seen most clearly in Central America, an area which historically has been the scene of internecine rivalry and warfare and which, until quite recently, has had many more dictators than democrats as national leaders. It is enlightening to glance at Central America's past history in contrast to its present performance.

In 1821 when Iturbide announced his plan for an independent Mexican empire and invited Central America to join it, most of the provinces accepted with alacrity. But parts of El Salvador, Nicaragua, and Honduras refused—until Iturbide, now known as Augustín the First, sent an army to convince them. But by the time that army had done its job, Emperor Augustín had abdicated; the result was the June 24, 1823, declaration of the Congress of Central American Provinces, declaring them free of Spain but bound as members of the *Provincias Unidas del Centro de América.*

By 1826, however, El Salvador had risen against the Federation President, Manuel José Arce, and was joined in 1828 by Honduras, Nicaragua, and Costa Rica. General Francisco Morazán led the Honduran forces into El Salvador, forcing the Federal troops to withdraw; then he marched on Guatemala City, capital of the Federation, capturing it on April 13, 1829. In 1830, Morazán became President of the Federation, ruling it with administrative wisdom but without corresponding democracy, under the system known as "liberal dictatorship."

In the succeeding several years, numerous armed uprisings broke out, the most serious and effective under the leadership of Rafael Carrerra. By 1838 it became apparent that the Federation could not endure, and by Act of Congress on May 18 of that year it officially committed suicide, allowing each member province to go its own way. To a great extent, the Central American republics have been going their own ways ever since —to the disadvantage of all.

Morazán became President of El Salvador in 1838, but was ousted in battle and exiled by Carrerra, who was then Guatemala's strong man. Morazán returned to Central America in 1842, overthrew Braulio Carrillo, the dictator of Costa Rica, and became President of that country, from which base he again set out to rebuild the Federation. But he was defeated by the other states, and, on September 15, 1842, he was shot.

The next year Honduras, El Salvador, and Nicaragua formed a new federation—which terminated in 1845 with war between Honduras and Nicaragua. Guatemala and El Salvador discussed federation that same year, but never got past the talking stage. El Salvador, Honduras, and Nicaragua sought federation in 1847, 1849, and 1862, always without success.

Then in 1876 delegates from all five Central American States sat down to hammer out a new understanding. Simultaneously, war broke out between Guatemala and El Salvador, ending the talks. Later attempts at union in 1895, 1907, and 1921 all failed, and the area remained fragmented.[2]

In recent years the entire political complexion of the area has brightened as old-style strong men gave way to freely elected leaders in virtually all countries. Under the subtle manipulation of several of these leaders, notably Dr. Ramón Villeda Morales of Honduras and General Miguel Ydígoras Fuentes of Guatemala, Central America today is closer to unity—permanent unity—than ever before in its history.

The rapprochement began with commercial agreements; a Central American common market, joint customs rulings and mutual exemptions, business freedom throughout the area for citizens of any one of the member countries, the founding of a Central American co-operative bank. Then joint sessions were held by Central American labor law experts to discuss uniform legislation in that area; by air travel specialists, to establish a central air traffic control facility; by radio men, to expedite that plan; by civil engineers, to consider uniform and co-ordinated methods of physical development.

Guatemala gave impetus to the new atmosphere of togetherness by founding a Central American normal school and awarding 50 scholarships in each country of the area; Honduras and Nicaragua by peacefully settling a 60-year-old border dispute involving some 7,000 square miles of coastal territory; El Salvador by declaring that whatever boundary disputes she might have with Honduras would assuredly be settled amicably.

Along with these developments, political and military unity began to emerge. The Organization of Central American States, formed in 1951 but long ineffectual, was restructured and strengthened. The foreign ministers of the member nations forged a new policy of mutual consultation—before any nation

[2] Although Secretary of State Elihu Root and President Theodore Roosevelt made beautiful speeches at a Washington conference on Central American Federation, the results of that meeting and of other attempts at union in the next ten years were nil—partly because of the U.S. "Big Stick" policy and our complete domination of Nicaragua during that period. See Salvador Mendieta, op. cit., Vol. II, pp. 28–105.

would make a political move that might affect any other it would be discussed by all concerned. These same foreign ministers consulted before the Punta del Este session in January 1962, and, at the meeting, presented a solidly united front. As this is written, discussions are under way for probable revival of the long-dead Central American Court of Justice, and plans are shaping up for a Joint Military Command under the OCAS.

Today, Guatemalan jelly jars bear labels reading "Consume What Central America Produces," and respected papers such as Honduras' *El Día* daily carry boldface fillers declaring "Central America Is One Country."

All of these developments were achieved while Costa Rica was led by President Mario Echandi, a conservative democrat whose attitude toward Central American federation was, at best, disinterested.

But as this is written, Costa Rica has a new President, Francisco J. Orlich, who declared himself for such unity within hours of receiving word of the election returns. (Orlich was the candidate of the National Liberation Party led by former President José Figueres, himself a dedicated federationist.) Thus chances today for the long-awaited Federation of Central American States are better than ever.

What does this mean in terms of hemispheric politics?

That the "postage stamp" nations whose voices often drowned each other out are achieving a position of stable unity from which they will talk in the councils of the world with new strength, just as the largest South American republics have been doing in the past few years.

This coalition, whether it reaches true federation or not, now presents an attractive natural partner to the rest of Latin America, establishing a geographical bridge between Mexico and South America and a psychological link among all the countries of Spanish speech.

That the Organization of American States will no longer be a creature of the United States, but a truly representative group in which the twenty Latin American nations will often vote together—and not always with the United States.

139

That the United States can no longer think of her southern neighbors as weak, disunited, poor cousins to be helped with charity and then commanded, but instead, must view them as potent in their own right, less developed than we but with a potential as great or greater than ours.

That Latin America, as an area already somewhat unified by social, religious, racial, and linguistic ties, once united politically will form a power bloc of formidable size and strength.

That we must deepen our understanding of the Indian mystique of much of Latin America, and the European heritage of the rest, and increase our *cultural* ties with the area. Indeed, we must accent such ties over and above the economic ones, both to indicate our awareness of values not measured in dollars and to counter the shrewd Communist line that says:

"The U.S. should be expelled from the inter-American system because it is not in tune with the cultural, social and indigenous melody of the Latin American nations."

Another dominant fact in Latin America today is the emergence of left-wing political parties that are against capitalism as well as communism and are already banded together in mutual help groups, such as the Inter-American Institute for Political Education in San José, Costa Rica, comprised of the following parties:

Acción Democrática (Venezuela; incumbent)

Frente Nacional Democrático and Partido Revolucionario Auténtico (Cuba)

Movimiento Nacionalista Revolucionario de Bolivia (incumbent)

Movimiento Revolucionario de Nicaragua

Partido Aprista Peruano (expected to win this year's elections)

Partido Liberación Nacional (Costa Rica; incumbent)

Partido Liberal de Colombia (incumbent)

Partido Liberal de Honduras (incumbent)

Partido Liberal Paraguayo and Partido Revolucionario Febrerista (Paraguay)

140

Partido Popular Democrático (Puerto Rico; incumbent)

Partido Revolucionario de Guatemala

Partido Revolucionario Dominicano and Vanguardia Revolucionaria Dominicana

Partido Socialista Ecuatoriano

Currently, most of the preceding parties that are in power are steering neutralist courses that neither follow the capitalist system nor the Communist way. Our tendency is to describe them as "leftist," or even as "Red-lining."[3] But more of these parties will come into power in the next year or so—especially in those countries still ruled by dictators where the liberal or revolutionary groups constitute the democratic vanguard and attract much support for their courage alone. We must, then, learn to live with them; indeed, we must be prepared to support them, if we are not to lose the friendship of Latin American governments just as we have lost that of many Latin American people.

Stemming from and, in turn, contributing to, the political liberalization of Latin America is a tremendous hunger for knowledge on the part of the ordinary people—the workers and farmers and students. Bookstores, formerly a rarity even in the cities, can be found everywhere today. And many of them sell inexpensive books, printed in Cuba, that spread the Communist line, while few handle the much more expensive U.S.-printed editions. The result is that millions of information-starved Latins are getting their first intellectual diet from, and in a form favorable to, the Communists.

We cannot combat this through official pamphlets issued by our U.S. Information Agency—these are quite uniformly dismissed as propaganda. Instead, we must devise a system under which our way of life as represented in literature receives fair treatment. This may well mean Federal subsidy for inexpensive

[3] Noting the label "Revolutionary," we react by assuming it means "Communist." It does not, in Latin America or elsewhere—and our semantic confusion causes many Latin non-Communist revolutionaries to believe that we distort the meanings of words just as much as the Russians do.

141

Spanish and Portuguese editions of U.S. fiction and nonfiction, and for their distribution through regular commercial channels throughout Latin America.

Concurrent with the search for information in Latin America is a new and stronger than ever awareness on the part of the people of the cultural strength of the area. Concerts, art exhibits, and lectures are more numerous than ever before, and better attended. Tegucigalpa, for example, a city poor even by Latin standards, has staged a half dozen major art exhibits within recent months, each of which has been better attended than the average game of *fútbol*. And spectators have walked away from each exhibit with fewer lempiras in their pockets and canvases under their arms. We seem largely unaware of this cultural renaissance, but if we are to understand Latin America today, it, too, must be taken into account, as I shall detail in the final chapter.

Internationally neutralist, internally unionist, commercially opportunist, intellectually hungry, and culturally alive—this is Latin America today. No easy place to make friends and influence people under the tired old policies we still have in effect—and no area to give up on, either. In the chapter that follows, I will attempt to outline some signposts for living in harmony with our southern neighbors, meanwhile helping them to help themselves.

12

Making Friends in Latin America

At the outset of this final chapter, let me admit that the job of helping Latin America and, at the same time making friends here, may be impossible. The history of our behavior here is an unfortunate one, and one which Latins rightfully resent. Perhaps it can be lived down, but not merely by large dollops of aid, and not overnight. The heart of the problem lies in the fact that North Americans seem more often than not to rub Latins the wrong way. This, too, can be changed, but not without major internal readjustments on our part.

Let's begin with people, since they are the heart of the matter. Toward the end of Chapter 7, I discussed some of the characteristics of "good gringos"; throughout the book I have been at pains to point out the traits of "bad" ones. Good sense and good manners could rub many of the rough edges off the latter, but deeper changes are required to create real rapport between gringo and latino.

First of all, any North American who really believes that he is better than anyone else just because he was born in the United States of America had better stay there; he'll only make enemies overseas, and his foreign experience will only serve to fortify his original prejudice, since travel is broadening only to people who are already fairly broad.

Secondly, no one should come here unless he has enough interest to learn something of the area—history, geography, culture, politics, customs—in advance, and to work in advance on the language. He need not speak the language well, but he must be prepared to speak it; he must be eager to do so, in

143

fact, out of his own desire to communicate as well as out of plain politeness.

Thirdly, any North American who comes here should want to learn as much as to teach, to receive as much as to give. We are a generous people, but our capacity for admitting need and for accepting gifts from others is remarkably low. Perhaps it is more blessed to give than to receive, but not when the giving is based on proud self-gratification ("See what I am doing for you!") and is accompanied by an arrogant refusal to receive.

Those of my compatriots who are accepted here and whom I mentioned in Chapter 7, were what I would call for want of a better term, "real people." These are the people who can live and be welcome anywhere; they are almost instantly recognizable. It is worth repeating that their "realness" stems from being individuals with a sense of personal identity and concomitant personal responsibility. I suspect that the need for an easy answer to the problem of identity underlies Latins' powerful family feeling just as it does our powerful organization manism—both the excessive family attachment and the excessive group attachment stand in the way of deep and meaningful human relations. It is notable that a Latin is never more offended than when a family member is attacked or criticized, while a North American rises more readily to the defense of his group—company or club or church—than he does to his own defense. (The mail I received after a certain article criticizing North American behavior here was evenly split: warm praise from individual North Americans writing as individuals, hot criticism from those writing as members of one or another group attacked in the article.)

One who accepts identification with group or family as the full answer to who he is becomes provincial; the person who is still in search of himself remains universal. It is, perhaps, the seeking and not the finding that counts, the ready eye and ear, the even readier head and heart. Seekers should come to Latin America; nonseekers, smug and complacent, should stay at home.

I know of no psychometric test to identify seekers, but, as

mentioned before, they are readily spotted in face-to-face encounters. (It may be that they can be isolated from their job applications: the fewer organizations in which they claim membership, the more chance that they have remained real people.) At any rate, this is the basic trait that government, industry, foundations, and the press should look for in the people they send here. It is, in practice, more important than degrees and technical skills; its lack in people otherwise qualified, lowers respect abroad both for North American degrees and skills.

Ideally, a North American working in Latin America should be rated on his personal relations as well as on his productivity, although the two will tend to equilibrium over time, I suspect. Those who fall short should be moved out before they can do further harm; those who fit in should be retained as long as they choose to stay. This, of course, runs counter to the rotation plan of our Foreign Service. My answer to this is to change the plan, for the simple reason that it does not work. Perhaps every Foreign Service officer dreams of becoming Ambassador to France, England, or Russia, for comfort, prestige, or for the challenge of the assignment, as the case may be. But there is equal comfort, and should be equal prestige, in cities like Mexico, Rio de Janeiro, and Buenos Aires—and the challenge of serving in Latin America, where North Americans are in as deep trouble as anywhere, seems to me well on a par with the Moscow post.

I do not believe that any magic formulas exist for good human relations in Latin America or anywhere else. And I do not see any real difference between Dale Carnegie's applied hypocrisy and the latest publications of the American Institute of Research for Peace Corps volunteers, *Working Effectively Overseas* and *Instructional Situations*—except that the Carnegie books were fairly well written. (Samples from *Working Effectively Overseas:* "One cannot avoid the requirement to motivate if one is to take a realistic view of the complexity of human affairs"; "Therefore it would be appropriate to give a neutral to positive assessment of the students' English in order to help the instructor with his own motivational problems.")

145

The key, although it sounds simple, is no pat formula. It lies in mutual need—the adjective as well as the noun is operative. As long as we believe that Latins need our help more than we need theirs, we will be arrogant; not until our dealings with them are based on our need as well as theirs will we be likable. (Robert Frost put it this way in "Two Tramps in Mud Time": "Only where love and need are one/ And the work is play for mortal stakes/ Is the deed ever really done/ For Heaven and the future's sakes.")

But even the best of personnel, motivated by the best attitudes and administering good policies, cannot hope for success if the environment within which they must work is so strongly anti-Yanqui that nothing they say or do is believed. Such is the condition in much of Latin America today. Our biggest chore is to change this; as we have seen, the Alliance for Progress, for all its twenty billions, has failed to do so.

Why?

Because it is silent on the main points of Latin resentment against us: our extractive industry here; our continued occupation of areas that Latins believe belong to them; our continuing aid to the military, historically a repressive force; our apparent intervention in local affairs through the use of technical experts in such sensitive areas as public security; the "boomerang effect" of much of our aid; the low quantity and poor quality of our press coverage of the area; the often ugly and usually unsuccessful behavior of our people here; the ignorance of Latin America on the part of our general public.

EXTRACTIVE INDUSTRY

Our first move, I believe, should be to create a loan fund from which Latin American governments or business firms may draw to begin buying our extractive industry in Latin America: the oil, mining, timber, and banana interests. To qualify for loans under this fund, governments would need to be stable and democratic; they and business firms would need to demonstrate their capacity to run the enterprise once they owned it. The loans should be interest-free, or at very low rates of interest, and should be administered by institutions such as the World Bank. Using these loans, the various democratic governments and local business interests would gradually buy up those North American interests which have created the greatest local friction, and for which the State Department has always been said, often incorrectly, to be working.

I grant that the mere availability of these funds would lead, in some cases, to expropriations. But there would be compensations and the operation would be a far cry from the wide-scale Cuban larceny. And frankly, I believe that expropriations are bound to come sooner or later in every country, just as they came in Cuba and in Mexico; better, then, to have them legal, orderly, compensated, and done with our help rather than over our protests.

This process would be lengthy; many of the governments and business firms in Latin America are far from being able to manage enterprises as huge and complex as some of our extractive interests here and will not attain the capability for some time to come. But the public relations benefits of the fund's creation would accrue from the first day of its announcement—for the very first time, Latins would believe in our sincerity. (Currently, with the *alianza*'s condemnation of *latifundios* coupled with its silence on the huge land holdings of U.S. companies, that sincerity remains in doubt.) Perhaps equally important, this move would pull the teeth from the Communist line with the deepest bite—that our only interest in this area is exploitative; that all our government operations here are aimed at protecting this huge investment and even huger return.

Simultaneously, we should announce a policy of support (through tax writeoffs and insurance against expropriation without dependency on bilateral accords) for all U.S. investment here in manufacturing and service industry—and none for new extractive enterprises. It would be feasible to allow lower premium rates on risk insurance and larger tax writeoffs for those firms whose ownership is jointly Latin and North American, pegging the scale to the degree of Latin participation in the management, direction, and profits of the enterprise. It is

147

demonstrable that joint operations are better risks (see Chapter 4); under current tax laws, income of U.S. citizens up to $20,000 a year and of Latins without limit remain untaxed: thus there is no conflict between this plan and good tax or insurance practice.

(A recommendation somewhat similar to that just suggested was made by Adolf Berle, one of our leading students of Latin America, and former Costa Rican President José Figueres, in a report submitted to the Second Inter-American Conference for Democracy and Freedom in April 1960. Although the report won the enthusiastic support of delegates ranging from Socialists to Christian Democrats (the upcoming political leaders in Latin America) we chose to ignore it.)

DISPUTED TERRITORY

If U.S. extractive enterprises are the major thorn in the side of sensitive, nationalistic Latins, certain of our government installations are almost equally painful. I think first of the Panama Canal, a source of embarrassment in recent times when the question of whose flag will fly there came up—and took entirely too long to be answered. Late in 1961, Panama's President Chiari asked for a new treaty on the Canal Zone that would recognize his country's "legitimate rights." Currently, we are paying Panama $1.93 million annually for the use of the canal; its control remains in our hands. Better by far to share with Panama on an equal basis: half the control and administration and half the receipts to each nation. The flags of the two countries could then fly side by side over a piece of land that is Panama's, administered happily in partnership with the United States.

In the case of the Swan Islands (see Chapter 3), I believe we should vacate them entirely, withdrawing all claims, however legally correct. Our presence there is odious to Hondurans and other Central Americans; our maintaining it provides more propaganda ammunition to the Communists; and we have no real use for the tiny islands anyway. Appealing to the International Court or other arbitration agency would only create further unpleasant publicity for us and further needless expense for Honduras. If we win the case, our image here will not improve; if we lose the islands, it would become even worse.

I also believe that headquarters of the Organization of American States should be moved from Washington to a more central and more Latin location: say San José, Costa Rica, or somewhere in Colombia. The psychological value of the move, with its recognition that the organization is more Latin than gringo, and its symbolism—the end of real or imputed U.S. domination of the group—would more than offset the expense of the move.

MILITARY AID

Since World War II, Latin America has spent more on munitions than it has on health, education, and development combined—a matter of over $2.5 billion! Latin America's standing armies total 500,000 men and cost over a billion dollars a year. But only five countries here have fought a foreign enemy in this entire century (and three of these supplied only token forces: Brazil in World Wars I and II, Mexico in World War II, and Colombia in the Korean War).

Mexico's army backed up the democratic forces during that country's revolution a half century ago; the armies of Brazil, Argentina, Venezuela, and Honduras have done the same more recently. But for the rest, the military in Latin America has been a repressive, antidemocratic force in most cases and a needless expense in all. Yet the Alliance for Progress says nothing about limiting military aid; that aid has, in fact, increased since the Kennedy Administration took office. For fiscal 1961, the United States allotted $9 million for Latin American navies against $3–4 million in earlier years; established an additional training center in the Canal Zone to teach guerrilla warfare; and the President authorized special arms shipments to Bolivia, Haiti, Ecuador, and El Salvador, on the basis of "defending democracy," although two of the then incumbent regimes had not been democratically elected and did not count on the support of their people.

Yet the leaders of Latin America have repeatedly stated their preference for economic rather than military aid; a House Subcommittee on Inter-American Affairs unanimously recommended (in the spring of 1959) that military aid gradually be eliminated; and the press here is all but unanimously against it. In the words of Ricardo Castro Beeche, editor of San José, Costa Rica's *La Nación:* "The sentiment created (by military aid) has been adverse; we would prefer not to receive it, since many of the governments have used these arms against their own people. It would be better to lose the friendship of a government that doesn't have the support of the people. This aid has been deplorable instead of beneficial. It has served only to create resentment against the U.S. for aiding governments that later launch attacks against their own people. . . ."

The major arguments advanced in favor of military aid here are that the military maintain stability, and that they can contribute to hemispheric defense in the event of outside attack.

Insofar as stability is concerned, Mexico, Costa Rica in Central America, and Uruguay in South America are without dispute the most stable and democratic countries of the southern half of the hemisphere. Mexico spends only 7 per cent of its budget on its 60,000 troops; Uruguay is lightly policed and has only 12,000 soldiers in all; Costa Rica maintains no army whatsoever.

As for hemispheric defense, how much can the aging, largely obsolete arms of Latin America really contribute in the event of nuclear war? Such a war would be fought with rockets and missiles, not with M-1's and F-86F Sabrejets. Meanwhile, our continuing military aid here earns enemies instead of friends, weakening our position in the war that is already underway— the Cold War.

TECHNICAL AID

We should also examine with new care our larger programs of technical aid in order to ascertain where and how they are serving to our own disadvantage. Technical aid is certainly doing no good in the case of police and military advisers, who are seen as interventionists by right and left wing alike, and whose presence here is taken advantage of by the Communists in their campaign of agitation. As noted in Chapter 6, it would be infinitely better to conduct such police and military courses Stateside, inviting Latin authorities to attend. It is, in fact, generally preferable that as much technical aid as possible be rendered in the States, thereby cutting down on our corps of representatives in Latin America (as of this writing, there are 79 in Honduras alone!) and equipping Latins to play the role of adviser to their own people.

Such a policy change would cause a great many more Latins to visit the United States. This is all to the good. First, because we as a people seem more comfortable and more effective as hosts than as guests (as noted earlier, we give better than we receive); second, because our firmest friends in Latin America are among those people who have spent some time Stateside. I have often heard such people defending gringos against blanket condemnation and carefully explaining that "they're not *all* like that; I've been there and I know."

Also as noted in Chapter 6, we would do well to recommend to Latin American governments needing individual consultants that they hire them from commercial consulting firms rather than get them from our government. Such commercial consultants serve rather than tutor Latins—and they pay full taxes and import duties, thereby avoiding the cries of "boomerang!" so often leveled against our government experts, who are usually exempt from such payments.

PRESS IMPROVEMENT

Insofar as North American ignorance of and disinterest in Latin America is concerned, two avenues of improvement exist: the schools and the press. There are excellent programs of Latin American studies in many of our universities, notably Stanford, UCLA, Texas, and Florida; these and others could do with significantly more support in the form of Federal schol-

151

arships and research grants, as could the better university foreign language programs, such as that at Purdue. Similar support should be given in the high schools for lower-level programs of study in Latin American history and geography, as well as Spanish and Portuguese. The availability of such scholarships and grants enhances the prestige of the subject matter, as we have learned recently in regard to the natural sciences. Greater knowledge of the language and broader acquaintance with the area academically will inevitably lead to deeper sympathy and more effective travel on the part of tourists and career people alike.

There is no precedent for, and there *is* potential danger in, Federal support of the press. Yet clear-cut need exists for improvement, quantitatively and qualitatively, of our coverage of this area. Why not a fund to be administered by, say, the Nieman Foundation or the Overseas Press Club, for the development of well-grounded Latin American correspondents? The mere existence of such personnel in no way assures that jobs will await them—but it does mean that those periodicals which do cover the area will do a better and more thorough job than they now do.

EDUCATING THE TOURIST

Tourists are tourists everywhere, and few of them make good representatives of the areas they come from. I've seen Latins in countries other than their own, or even in other parts of their own country, acting just as ugly and thoughtlessly as any gringo. We cannot expect that our tourists will really do us much good here but we can try to avoid at least some of the harm they cause. A straightforward booklet accompanying every passport issued for Latin America—not the double talk prepared for Peace Corps personnel, but a terse, honest account of how we look in Latin eyes—stands at least some chance of bettering the situation. One's interest in an area is never higher than when preparing to visit there; any informative material issued along with a passport would be avidly read and, if properly prepared, could have significant effect. It will not create tact or common sense where they do not already exist. But it might well alert tactful, sensible people to possible embarrassments for themselves and for their country they otherwise might blunder into.

Withdrawing from contested territories, handing over control of our extractive industries, placing less emphasis on military aid, distributing technical aid more carefully, and improving our press coverage and our knowledge of the area—all this can eliminate many of the complaints against us here. Certainly all of these programs are necessary adjuncts to the Alliance for Progress. Indeed, the Alliance has little or no chance of succeeding unless accompanied by these measures.

And one more.

Throughout this book I have stressed the importance of the intellectual in Latin America: far from being an ivory tower recluse, he is a political activist. Intellectuals govern most Latin American countries today; intellectuals who oppose them will govern tomorrow.

I have also pointed out how the Latin intellectual becomes, first, anti-Yanqui, and then, in reaction, pro-Communist.

THE INTELLECTUALS

Why not, then, a program aimed at winning friends among the intellectuals? Most of them wear frayed collars and out-of-style suits as a virtual badge of office: local support is all but nonexistent. And most of them would be extremely grateful for any support that had no strings attached.

Currently, we are spending some money (although not much) for performances in Latin America by several of our entertainers. This effort has no real meaning, since the performers do not serve as good will ambassadors, and, as for showing off our talent, prints of Hollywood movies do a better job more cheaply. We might better invest this money in fellowships for Latin American poets, novelists, musicians, and painters to study in the States or elsewhere, and for support after their academic studies end. I envision lifetime grants in outstanding cases. The results would more than repay the expense in terms of good will, since intellectuals are so potent and prestigious here politically.

We would thus be demonstrating that our interests go beyond the material; we would be heightening interest in Latin America among our own people, since many of the grantees would go to the States to study, lecture, and perform; we would be making a signal contribution to a society that urgently seeks cultural advance even under conditions that stringently limit economic development.

Honduran painter Mario Castillo, one of the hemisphere's most promising young artists, told me once, "The future of many of our countries lies in cultural rather than material things. Industrialization is just too difficult in many cases—and it runs against the grain of our personality. But imagine these countries making their unique contribution in art and music and literature!" Then he grinned ruefully and added, "But there just isn't any money." There could be, if we supplied it. And the potential results in terms of our relations here are as exciting as those in terms of Latin America's own development as envisioned by my friend Mario.

A NEW START IN FOREIGN POLICY

As Edmund Stillman and William Pfaff point out, the United States is still operating under a set of ideas originated and first applied in 1947, while the world has changed radically since that time.[1]

The most radical change is the emergence of new, hungry nations and a new attitude on the part of older hungry nations —an attitude that resists the United States as well as Russia, that seeks for each republic, however tiny and weak, its own place in the sun. This change has eliminated the old bipolar

[1] Edmund Stillman and William Pfaff, "A New Start in Foreign Policy," *Harper's*, January 1961.

world in which one was either with us or with the Russians; our influence and theirs is shrinking, and the influence of the smaller nations, especially those which have joined together in blocs, is growing.

We saw clear-cut evidence of this change in the Punta del Este meetings early in 1962, when the biggest Latin American nations voted against the United States on direct individual action against the Castro regime. Although juridical considerations were stressed by these negative nations, we can and should see their action as a manifestation of the rejection of the bipolar concept: they are not prepared—or, better said, are no longer ready, to back us completely.

It is also notable that most of the South American governments consulted with each other before going to Punta del Este, as did the Central American governments. This move, plus the several moves toward unity in Central America noted in Chapters 5 and 11, is indicative of a growing awareness among Latin American leaders that their area, if formed into a political bloc, can have new potency in the councils of the world.

In the face of these growing tendencies in Latin America, the very name, "Alliance for Progress," is an unfortunate choice. Latin leaders and their people do not seek alliances, either with us or with the Russians; they seek their own way. Equally mistimed and unfortunate is the new wave of tough talk on the part of such formerly liberal voices as *The Reporter*'s Max Ascoli. If Latin America is moving toward neutralism as a policy and unity as a technique, the disparagement of neutrals is the most reactionary and least attractive attitude we might adopt.

As Stillman and Pfaff emphasize: "Our interest lies with the growth of authentic states capable of looking after their own affairs, responsive to their own needs and character, willing to take a responsible role in the concerns of their regions. Such states need not be allied to us, or even be especially friendly, so long as there are enough of them to assure that no single

155

power or combination of powers can enforce dominance in the world."[2]

To recognize that our interest is as these authors see it requires not only a shift in policy but also in fundamental attitude. We must lose the futile and arrogant sense of destiny under which we have usurped responsibility for the whole world. Our responsibility is more modest than this, and, as recent events have proven, our hopes for achievement must be more modest than this. Indeed, as pointed out in Chapter 7, we still have many fences to mend at home.

After fifteen years of dedicated, often sanctimonious effort, the Cold War remains at a stalemate. After fifteen years of dollar diplomacy on the widest scale in history, we have failed to buy any friends, just as Russia's ruble diplomacy has bought none. It is time to question, not whether our effort has been too little but whether it has not been too big; it is time for modesty and humility, not for further world-wide paternalism.

Walter Lippmann, speaking of our relations with Latin America, once noted that we were most liked and respected here in times when we were "the least smug about our own affairs and the least satisfied with ourselves"—the Wilson days and those of the two Roosevelts.[3] And we were, in those days, at our most effective internationally. In human terms, this is entirely understandable: smugness and complacency are universal targets for attack, while humility calls out for affection. Today, after a brief spate of self-criticism, we seem to be returning to a new wave of bragging and self-congratulation, a new outbreak of condescension toward the world. Nothing could be more destructive of our relations here and elsewhere, or more inappropriate at this time.

It is true, of course, that great causes tend to become obsolete, leaving the world with a sense of wonder that it ever could have been so involved with them in the first place. The long view would indicate that this will happen—indeed, is hap-

[2] Op. cit.

[3] *Sic:* I cannot agree with his statement as to the first Roosevelt (see Chapter 2), but the point in general is well taken.

156

pening—in the Cold War between the United States and Russia. The emergence of new nations and their combination into power blocs robs the big struggle of much of its bigness; Russia is challenged now by China, we by several of our old allies, including Great Britain and France and, more and more, Latin America.

History teaches humility, if it teaches anything at all; time changes all things, even the overweening power of the United States. And in all humility, we cannot look on Latin America and much of the rest of the world as weak and incapable of taking care of itself, nor can we see our helping hand as the whole foundation of world development.

Greater humility on the part of our leaders, political and intellectual, will soon filter down to our public: the mood of the times is the product of such men, just as their emergence to leadership is the result of earlier moods. The North American under Franklin Roosevelt *felt* differently about Latin America than he has since—and this different feeling, as much as any other factor, contributed to our relative popularity here during the Good Neighbor years.

We are just as nationalistic as the Latin Americans; North Americans appear, down here, a good deal the way Texans appear at home: big and loud, albeit not without charm. It is natural to feel that one's birthplace is the best and that its products, ranging from automobiles to people, are the greatest. It is also provincial, inaccurate, and worth growing out of in a world as small and cross-linked as that of today. We have our strengths and our weaknesses; the recognition of and an attempt to overcome the latter is the only real way of demonstrating and finding acceptance for the former.

Despite the deep vein of anti-Yanqui feeling here, many Latin Americans want to like and respect us, our way of life, and our products. I have heard vociferously anti-gringo merchants wax enthusiastic over an "American fabric," an "American jam," or "American automobiles," implying or even stating that they were the best because made in the United States of America. I have heard avowed *fidelistas* talk yearningly of going to

157

the States, to visit or to live. I have had any number of Latins ask me, with fervid curiosity, how we do one or another thing back home, assuming always that we do it better.

These are tendencies that arrogance and condescension can kill, but that humility can cultivate. Not to make Latin Americans "just like us"—they don't want to be, can't be, and shouldn't be—but just to make them like us.

As a gringo who has lived with Latin Americans in good times and bad, in good places and bad, I can testify that one could not have better friends.

Index

Bates, Marston, 72, 73, 115
Batista, Fulgencio, 26, 28–30, 40, 85, 96
Beltrán, 124
Berle, Adolf, 56, 148
Bertrand, Ernesto Vitori, 106
Beryllium, 5
Betancourt, Rómulo, 67
Blas, 8
Bolívar, Simón, 21, 30, 109
Bolivia, 4
  attitude toward Cuba, 133
  Communists in, 21, 110, 134
  cultures in, 6
  economics of, 127
  language in, 15
  military in, 149
  news coverage of, 60, 67
  political parties in, 140
  population growth in, 117
Bonilla, Manuel, 54–55
Borges, Jorge Luís, 8
Braden Copper Co., 49, 50
Brandon, Henry, 60, 61
Brasilia, 115
Brazil, 4
  attitude toward Cuba, 133, 134
  arts in, 8, 9, 14, 85
  Communists in, 110, 135
  government in, 18
  industries in, 18, 50–51, 57, 68
  language in, 14, 15
  military in, 149
  news coverage of, 60, 66, 68
  oil companies in, 113
  population in, 18, 119
  at Punta del Este, 21
  research in, 10
  trade with, 25
Brinton, Crane, 89
Brown and Root, 75
Bryan-Chamorro Treaty, 33
Buenos Aires, 8, 16

Bueso Arías, Jorge, 95
Businessmen, 48–58

Cáceres Lara, Victor, 24
California University, Los Angeles, 151
Campesinos, 21, 87
Canal Zone, 148, 149
Caracas, 110
Carías, Gonzalo, 104
Carías, Marco, 104
Carías, Tiburcio, 104
Caribbean area, language in, 15
Carnauba wax, 5
Carnegie, Dale, 90, 145
Carrerra, Rafael, 137
Carrillo, Braulio, 137
Carrión, Benjamin, 102
Caso, Alfonso, 7, 10
Castañeda Batres, Oscar, 102
Castillo, Mario, 8, 154
Castro, Fidel, 21–22, 29, 37, 38, 46, 59, 65, 95, 96, 102, 124, 127, 133, 135, 155
Castro, Raúl, 97
Castro Beeche, Ricardo, 150
Catholicism, 16–17, 120, 121
Celanese, 48
Central America, art appreciation in, 14
  communists in, 94, 104–107
  Congress of University Students, 97
  correspondents in, 60, 61–62
  cultures in, 6
  history of, 136–139
  industrialization in, 51–54, 116
  language in, 15
  United Provinces of, 36
  unity in, 155
  Unity Party in, 33
Central American Court of Justice, 32, 33, 139

El Salvador—(*Continued*)
  population in, 18
  protests against U.S., 33
  religion in, 17
Ellender, Allen J., 41, 42
Evans, Rowland, 117
Excelsior, 8
Existentialism, 88, 92
Exports from Latin America, 5
Expropriations, 147
Extractive industries, 49, 52, 58,
  126, 146–148

Failures in Latin America, 19–
  34
Falk, Carlos, 96
Family attachments, 11, 144
Federation of Central American
  States, 137–139
Federation of University Stu-
  dents, 38, 96, 97
Figueres, José, 66, 88, 125, 139,
  148
Fischer, John, 83
Florida University, 151
Foreign policy of U.S., 154–158
Foreign Service, 45–46, 145
Fortune, 54
Franco, 40, 80, 83–84
Freyre, Gilberto, 8
Frost, Robert, 146
Fruit companies, 54–56, 102
  (*see also* United Fruit)

Galbraith, John Kenneth, 10, 80
Gamio, Manuel, 10
García, J. Urciel, 10
García Peña, Roberto, 42
Gardner, Arthur, 40
Gaucho stories, 24
Gibraltar Shipping Co., 37
Goulart, João, 134, 135
Government, attitude toward,
  107–108
  forms of, 17–18

Government—(*Continued*)
  by Incas, 7
  political parties in, 140
Grace, W. R., 132
Granada, 9
Great Stories of all Nations, 89
Gringa, La, 24
Gringos, feelings against, 19–34
Guajiros, 21
Guantánamo Bay, 28
Guaraní, 15
Guatemala, 4
  Communists in, 21, 94, 105–
    107, 109, 110, 134
  correspondents in, 8, 60
  cultures in, 6
  government in, 65
  language in, 15
  political parties in, 141
  revolution in, 56
  tax legislation in, 126
  United Fruit in, 51
Guatemala City, 137
Guayijíqui Indians, 16
Guevara, 134
Guitar music, 9
Guzmán, Martín Luís, 8

Hagras, Ibrahin, 97
Haiti, 4, 33, 149
Harper's, 46, 48, 83, 129
Harza, 75
Hasbun, 96
Havana Conference, 34 (*see
  also* Cuba)
Hay-Herrán treaty, 32
Haya de la Torre, Victor Raúl,
  135
Heidegger, 88
Henequén, 5
Henríquez Ureña, Pedro, 7, 15
Hernández, José, 24, 86
Herrera, Felipe, 119
Herrera, Sarbelio, 105
Herter, Christian, 37, 38

Roosevelt, Theodore, 32, 98, 138, 156
Root, Elihu, 32, 138
Rusia, 84
Rusk, Dean, 127
Russell, Bertrand, 88
Russia, 3 (*see also* Communism)

Sabogal, 8
San José, Costa Rica, 32, 140, 150
San Pedro, 77, 95, 96, 99, 100
San Pedro Sula, 72
San Salvador, Communists in, 104
Sánchez, Florencio, 24
Sánchez, Moisés, 130
Santa Ana, Communists in, 104
Santa Tecla, Communists in, 104
Santiago, Chile, 8, 31, 33
Santo Domingo (*see* Dominican Republic)
São Paulo, 18
Sartre, Jean-Paul, 88, 92
Saturday Review, 60
Saxons, 79, 86
Schools, Latin American studies in, 151–152
Scientific research projects, 10
Sears, Roebuck & Company, 57
Segovia, 9
Shearer, John C., 50, 51
Shell, 48
Siguatepeque, 77
Sinclair, 48
Siqueiros, 8, 116
Sisal, 5
Slavery, 27, 79
Smith, Earl E. T., 40, 59
Sodium nitrate, 5
Somoza, Anastasio, 40, 46, 66, 85
Somoza, Luís A., 94
Sonata de Estió, 86
Sorhegui, Silvio, 98

Soviet Encyclopedia, 109
Spanish-American War, 3, 28, 32
Spanish Civil War, 83
Spanish culture, 7
Spanish language, 4, 14–16, 45, 89, 152
Spanish rule of Cuba, 27
Speech zones in Latin America, 15–16
Sperm whale oil, 5
Standard Fruit Co., 102
Standard Oil Co., 24
Stanford University, 151
Stevenson, Adlai, 20, 21, 88
Stillman, Edmund, 154, 155
Stroessner, 66
Sugar, 5, 29, 41
Swan Islands, 35, 60–61, 108, 127, 148–149

Tabasco, State of, 17
Talanga, 104
Tamayo, 8
Tantalum, 5
Teachers' United Front, 105
Technical cooperation, 70–78, 103, 150–151
Tegucigalpa, 35, 39, 54, 64, 95, 99, 100, 103, 104, 111, 142
Tela, 65
Tela Railroad Co., 52, 53
Telles, Raymond L., 45
Tello, Julio C., 10
Territory disputes, 148–149 (*see also* Swan Islands)
Texas Petroleum, 48
Texas University, 151
Theater productions, 24
Time, 19, 20, 43, 60, 62–68, 108
Tin, stockpiled, 127
Tortured Ones, The, 24
Tourists, 76–78, 152–153
Toynbee, Arnold, 79, 115

169

D. H. RADLER

a resident of Latin America since 1958, and a correspondent on the area for a number of U.S. newspapers, magazines, and news services (The Washington *Post;* San Francisco *Chronicle; Newsweek;* Medical World News; World-Wide Medical News Service; McGraw-Hill World News), brings to his interpretation of our image in Latin America a unique background of education, experience, and insight.

Born in New York City in 1926, he began to learn French almost simultaneously with English, developing an interest in languages that underlies his current polylingual skill (he speaks Spanish, Portuguese, Italian, and Japanese as well as French and English). He studied languages academically, first at DeWitt Clinton High School, and Cheshire Academy, and then as an undergraduate at Kenyon College. He learned Japanese in the U.S. Army specialized training program in World War II. His major assignment, however, was as a psychometrist in the Ninth Service Command, and his graduate work, at the University of Chicago, was in psychology and related social and biological sciences.

In 1958 an assignment to set up a hemisphere-wide research information service in Spanish and English for the United Fruit Company took him and his family to Latin America where they have lived ever since. Mr. Radler has traveled extensively in a dozen Latin-American countries, not just in the capitals but in the mountains and jungles, the lakes and the deserts. He has also served as a teacher in Latin-American high schools, from which, he reports, he learned much more than he taught.